To KALA,

LOTS OF L

X

A big thank you for buying this book!
I hope that you'll enjoy reading it as much as
we've all enjoyed writing it for you.
Kinky Boots is still running strong
because of your ongoing support!

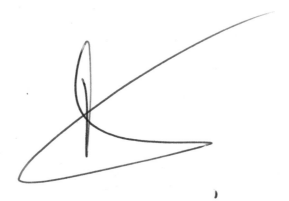

Steve Pateman
The Kinky Boot Man
Twitter: @KinkyBootMan
Facebook: Boss in Boots – Steve Pateman
Instagram: stevepateman.bossinboots
Website: www.bossinboots.co.uk

(Proudly) First self-published in 2018.

www.bossinboots.co.uk

Copyright © Steve Pateman 2018.
bossinboots.stevepateman@gmail.com

ISBN   978-1-5272-2970-9

A copy of this book is available from The British Library.

Printed and bound by Print2Demand Ltd.
www.print2demand.co.uk

Designed and typeset by Daniel Kemshed.
DK- Websites, Media & Marketing

ACKNOWLEDGEMENTS

My heartfelt thanks go out to the following for their help,
support and guidance.

Wilson Browne Solicitors: an award-winning law firm with nationally
recognised expertise in helping businesses and individuals. Thanks to Andrew
Kerr, Guy Zarins, Kevin Rogers and all the team for their help, legal advice
relating to the publication of this book and other matters. Their friendly,
down to earth approach and supportive nature was received with gratitude.

Also, to Wayne Jenkins and the marketing team for their sponsorship and
support with marketing ideas, materials and photography.

www.wilsonbrowne.co.uk

Gavin Wallace, for providing such excellent publicity photos and imagery for
the book, also for his contribution and help with the design elements.
Working under pressure and to a tight schedule he has worked miracles.
Gavin's worked with many big-name DJs, celebrities, top magazines and won
many awards. He also provides corporate photography to many other clients
such as; BBC, Sony Music (US & UK), Columbia as well as numerous local
businesses

www.gavinwallacephotography.co.uk

All of those mentioned have contributed their time, expertise, and support
willingly and enthusiastically, for which I offer my sincerest thanks.

WELCOME

My name is Steve Pateman. I'm a firefighter in Northampton, right in the heart of England. This wasn't always my job. No, once I ran a shoe factory doing what Northamptonshire has always done the best; I made boots and shoes.

Then I was featured in an article in a national newspaper and that led to the BBC making a programme about my factory. From then on, my life began to take some of the most incredible and unexpected twists and turns imaginable!

Follow me on a journey of discovery, a hidden world of erotica, of laughter, of embarrassment and of the wonderful customers and characters who would change my life for ever.

You may not realise it but it's a story you probably know already. It's a story known by millions round the world thanks to a name change, a slight hotting-up of the facts and a series of things that happened: two BBC2 TV documentaries, a major box-office hit movie and a Tony Award winning musical.

FOREWORD

So here it is, at long last: my book! After a television programme, a film and then a musical, the only thing missing from the set was this book. Follow me on my journey that starts in an ordinary shoe factory in the back streets of Earls Barton and leads me through fun and laughter, tears and sadness into an amazing, outrageous world of glitz, glamour and show biz.

A series of events, (some would say fate), took me to another way of life and of experiences that changed my outlook on life forever. If, like me, you were slightly naïve to some parts of society, follow my clumsy, awkward, embarrassing moments; laugh with me or at me. I hope you enjoy the stories and anecdotes of the 'behind the scenes' nuts and bolts story.

Now forever called 'The Kinky Boot Man" and known for being the boss who shaved his legs and learnt to walk in six-inch heels, this is my story of notoriety or, dare I say, 'fame'. My thanks go out to the most wonderful people, characters, customers and now friends who have made my story. Their kindness, acceptance, sense of humour and tolerance are a lesson to us all. Without them my story would be meaningless and empty. My only regret is, I wish I had discovered this new world 20 years earlier.

So many other people deserve my thanks: my workforce at WJ Brookes, my family, my friends, my new work colleagues in the Fire Brigade and, more than anyone, my long-suffering wife, Sara. She has stood by me through all these trials and tribulations, my crazy ideas AND my commitment to making this project work.

Additionally, she supported despite the long hours, the lost weekends, the travel and my appearances on TV; not to mention the lost time I sacrificed with her, and the early years I lost at home with our son, Dan.

To Sara and Dan; I thank you for your understanding. I hope you forgive me, especially for embarrassing you so often in my boots on TV. Finally, to my author, scribe and friend, David Saint, who took up the challenge of putting my ramblings, stories and anecdotes into a fantastic book, which I have so enjoyed doing.

To everyone who has been involved in the story of The Kinky Boot Factory and Kinky Boots, however large or small the part you played, your help was invaluable, and I thank you all most sincerely.

Steve Pateman
The Kinky Boot Man

6

PREFACE

In his Foreword, Steve keenly tells you about his journey that took him from an office above a shoe factory in Earls Barton, Northamptonshire, England to the glittering world of show-biz. I have to say that, in writing this book with him, I have in some way shared that journey and living through Steve's memories has been an exciting experience.

Many people who read this book will do so as a result of their enjoyment watching the remarkable stage musical version of Steve's life in Cyndi Lauper and Harvey Fierstein's wonderful 'Kinky Boots' that has wowed audiences worldwide. Others might have come by way of Julian Jarrold's brilliant 2005 film, 'Kinky Boots', that starred Chiwetel Ejiofor, Joel Edgerton, Nick Frost, Linda Bassett, Sarah-Jane Potts and Jemima Rooper. A few might even remember the BBC2 TV documentary, 'Trouble at The Top', the programme that really started Steve's journey back in February 1999.

May I welcome you to this book and hope you enjoy your journey with Steve. However, there are one or two important points I feel I must make to help and clarify your understanding of what follows. As you must realise, the English language is ever changing, and that means that many of the terms we use every day change as well. This book deals with a world that is largely unknown to the vast majority of people round the globe.

'Divine' footwear was aimed initially at one certain market, and here is the first term that has changed; that market involved 'transvestites'. Having taken professional advice, I understand this is a term that is now largely avoided in favour of the term, 'cross-dressers'.

Naturally the boots and shoes also appealed to another market: that of people undergoing or considering gender reassignment. Once the term 'tranny' was used, this is now understandably regarded as not politically correct and has been replaced by the simple and all-embracing term, 'trans', that also includes cross dressers. Present throughout is another, very different, group largely involving the gay community, that of drag artistes, men who cross-dress outrageously mostly for entertainment purposes.

I want to make it clear that in this book, Steve and I have been diligent in not confusing these three groups. We have no intention of insulting or vilifying anyone. Indeed Steve and, to a lesser extent, I have come to know, befriend and understand a great many of these wonderful people and without them, this book would not have been written.

David Saint 2018

I dedicate this book to all those that have put up with me, for all these years.

Sara and Dan Pateman.

Margaret and Richard Pateman.

Friends, Family, Work Colleagues at W. J. Brookes Ltd and those of the Fire Brigade.

*And finally,
I especially wish to thank David Saint for the realisation of this book.*

CHAPTERS

I

Out of the Blue

"Steve, there's a possible new customer on the phone, she's..." said Rosie, one of the ladies in the office.
"Brilliant! Fantastic! Put her through," I said.
"But there's something you need to know about this customer, she's..."
"Rosie, there's nothing you need to tell me, it's a customer. Put the call through."

Things were tough, really tough. At that moment I needed every new customer I could get.

She put her through. I suppose I was expecting the usual sort of caller, probably a secretary who'd announce a company name and then put me through to her boss; that's what normally happened, but to my surprise, on the line was a deep, rich, cultured voice announcing herself as Sue Sheppard of 'Lacies-Fantasy Girl' of Folkestone.

"Do you, or can you make ladies footwear?"
"I'm sorry," I replied, a bit disappointed, "unfortunately we're a men's or unisex manufacturer".
"That's OK, I'm looking for men's footwear." she said.

Hang on. At this point I was thinking, where's this going? We either make men's or we make ladies, what does she want? I was intrigued.

"Tell me more about it."
Then she came out with it. "I'm interested in sourcing court shoes, ankle boots, knee boots and thigh boots, all in men's sizes."

By now my mind had gone into overdrive! Why? What for? And to do what with?? I was trying to understand what she'd said. This was something rather new in the backstreets of our village hearing someone talk about high-heeled footwear for men!

"So you want ladies footwear in men's sizes?"
"Yes. P'raps I'd better explain. You see we're what we call a changing centre, a cross-dressing store on the South Coast."
"And that means?" I was, after all, just an innocent boot-maker!
"Well, our customers can't get good quality boots and shoes in their sizes".

After a bit of crafty digging I found out that Sue ran, and still does run, a place where cross-dressers could go for a complete outfit. They could select from a range of wigs; buy make-up, choose from a wide variety of dresses, from a party frock to a ball gown. They'd complete the look with a nice pair of shoes or boots. And that, it seemed, was the problem. The footwear.

When I asked her if it was a very small industry she said, "Far from it, dah-ling, you'd be surprised. It's quite a secret world you know, we have to be the soul of discretion, but we have hundreds of men who love the thrill of cross-dressing. We can manage the wigs and the frocks, but can we get people who can make the fab sexy boots and shoes? The demand far outstrips the supply and that's why I've come to you".

This was getting interesting. Sue went on, "The main problem is the fitting dah-ling. It's terrible; men are obviously heavier than women, and specially heavier on the footwear." She let out a heartfelt sigh. "We get loads of customers coming back saying the heels have snapped, and anyway you should see a fifteen-stone builder trying to force his foot into a ladies shoe, it can cause real problems."

By now my head was spinning with visions of Cinderella's ugly sisters cutting their toes off to get their feet into glass slippers!

"And the real trouble is", she said, becoming more passionate, "all the boots and shoes we sell are just ladies styles made in bigger sizes and that just doesn't work. When it comes to fitting, men's legs are different from ladies. We need boots made specially for men."

It was too good a challenge to ignore. I had to give it some serious thought. Could there really be a gap in the market for this?

"Sue, if we could get the fitting right and solve the problem of breaking heels," I asked, "what else could we do?"

She was very concerned about the delivery time; she wanted them as soon as we could make them. No pressure there then!

"Surely there must be someone who manufactures these shoes and boots already?" I was really curious.
"Most often I have to wait for six to eight months for delivery."
"Well," I said, "we make 4,000 pairs of shoes a week, so delivery isn't a problem."

I was really growing more and more interested. I rashly suggested we could probably deliver in six to eight weeks. She was over the moon.

Her next important demand was quality. I assured her that wouldn't be a problem. I told her that we were both a British Safety Standard 5750 Kitemark and an approved CE company. She asked what that was. So I explained that The Kitemark was the forerunner of the CE mark, an assurance of quality. I let her know that we'd worked for some of the major catalogue companies and that we had strict internal quality control. I could hear her almost purring with satisfaction!

Last of all was the price. Now, I know full well that every new customer wants to screw the price down to get the best product for the lowest amount. So it was a shock when Sue said, "If you can get all the other bits right, the price isn't a major issue. If you can deliver the best quality in the time you promise, you can name your price."

"Wow! That's music to my ears!" I hoped I didn't sound too enthusiastic, but I was.

Now one thing I haven't yet revealed is that we were desperate for customers. For reasons I'll go into later, the boot and shoe industry was going through a really hard time. In fact, our company was on the brink of disaster. We faced a bleak future knowing that we'd possibly have to cut down on staff, and then, if the worst came to the worst, we'd have to call it a day and close the factory.

However outrageous this new chapter in my life sounded, it could be our lifeline. It was make or break. I had to say yes. I had to go for it! What did I have to lose? Was it worth a try? We were bound to face difficulties and problems, but surely nothing I couldn't overcome. But would my workforce play ball?

Bouncing up and down in my chair, I was thinking, this could be good, this could help to save the factory. But we in the shoe trade know that not everything is as good as it sounds. So, reality kicked in for a moment.

Trying to sound every inch the serious businessman I said to Sue, "Well, I really think I need to do a bit of research, talk to a few people, work out the implications." It would involve a huge investment and I would have to make sure it was worth it. "Are there any other people I could talk to," I continued, "just to see exactly how wide the interest could be?"

"Of course dah-ling, I can give you a load of contacts, just tell them I sent you. As you can imagine, it's a very close-knit business, we all know each other and we all try to work with others in the trade, being part of the so-called 'sex industry'." Oh My God! She'd said it! I went hot and cold. That little three-letter word had hit me right between the eyes.

Sex. Sex. Sex.

I clapped my hand over the phone glancing around to make sure no one had heard that three-letter word! After all, this was Earls Barton and I was tinkering with an industry I knew nothing about. I was a shoemaker. Could I, little old me, get involved in 'THE SEX INDUSTRY'!!!?? What was I getting myself into…???

I told her I'd have to get back to her. She purred again and said she looked forward to hearing from me soon. "If you can say yes, that would be heavenly. I'm sure you won't regret it."

It was time for a strong cup of tea and time to think. So I spent the next hour on the phone ringing each of the ten people she'd told me about. I told them "Sue sent me!" and explained what it was all about.

"If we could get the quality, delivery, fitting and the price right would you be interested in buying from us?"
The unanimous response was, "Yes, the shoes complete the look. We're crying out for someone who could make them for us."

The idea was born. My head was buzzing and spinning at the possibilities. I needed to find out more about this secret world I was about to throw myself in to.

I told Rosie and Clarice to hold my calls and take messages; something important had come up.

Without delay I left the office, jumped into my car and started for home. Then, wondering, I thought, "Why waste a minute"? First stop, our local shop. The same shop I went into every morning to pick up my paper. They all knew me well in there; I'd been a regular customer for years.

It was one of those occasions when you're so focussed on the task at hand that your mind is elsewhere. Without another thought I went straight over and reached up to the top shelf of the magazine rack and took every glossy girlie mag there was. I was a man on a mission! I took one after another and piled them up on my arm. I went straight to the counter to pay for my rather large selection of soft porn!

That's when I realised what I was doing! I stopped. Paused. Took my wallet out and looked at the face of the pretty girl behind the counter; the one who served me every day with my newspaper and half pound of chocolate raisins. She looked at me straight in the eye and glanced up and down seeing this pile of magazines sitting in front of me. Her smiling eyes met mine and she said, "Looks like you're in for a hard night Steve!?"

It's at moments like this that you hope the floor would open up and swallow you. I made some gurgling noises that vaguely resembled speech and blurted out, "It's a special project I'm thinking about." A knowing grin crept across her face. She laughed and looked at my scarlet cheeks. "I've heard it called many things in my time, but never a 'special project'". I hurriedly paid and ran out of the shop.

Safely home and still glowing scarlet from the embarrassing first encounter with my new way of life, I ran into the house, dumped the magazines on the table, ripped open the covers and started going through them. I wanted to see what the models were wearing on their feet.

Unfortunately, the bit that I wanted to see was from the thighs downwards, whereas the magazines were only interested in the thighs upwards!!! Still it was a worthwhile exercise. At least I'd had a glimpse of the market I was aiming at.

A sudden thought flashed across my mind. Why limit the footwear to men? These magazines showed mostly women. If they bought kinky footwear as often as my wife buys ordinary shoes: WOW, the possibilities could be endless.

Then I thought of another avenue to explore. In those days there were adverts in the weekend papers inviting you to send a stamped addressed envelope for catalogues packed with sexy underwear and fetish items for men and women. Of course they weren't in the business of selling common or garden Y-fronts. Their men's selection featured brightly coloured skin-tight satin briefs at one end of the scale and black leather ones complete with zips in all the right places at the other.

Naturally I needed to send off for a few of those as part of my education. I collected all the weekend papers, sent the obligatory stamped addressed envelope and looked forward with anticipation to their arrival. Thank goodness they would arrive in plain brown envelopes!!!!

A few days later our regular postman, who just happened to be one of my old school mates, came with a wad of brown envelopes. I was just rushing out of the house.

"Steve I've got a bit of post for you."
"Oh thanks Pete, I'm in a bit of a rush now, push them through the letter box I'll look at them tonight."

He was no fool. He knew exactly what was in the envelopes. He handed me the post and I grabbed it as we played a mini tug-of-war. When I looked at him questioningly as to why he wouldn't let go, he nodded and winked at the top envelope and said, "Amazing what you learn about people from a postmark, especially as I had one of these catalogues the other day."

He turned and walked away, laughing and chuckling to himself. He had that "I've got another good story to tell the lads down the pub tonight" air about him.

For the second time in a matter of days, that overpowering feeling of embarrassment grabbed me yet again. I made a mental note. "If this is going to happen all the time, I've got to overcome my embarrassment; it's only work after all!"

These brochures were just another part of my education into my new line of business. But there was still so much more that I needed to know if I were to make a success of it: more input; more insight; more understanding. It was still a world that was completely alien to me.

Even though the magazines and brochures had been informative, they still hadn't hit the spot. I still needed more information and research. One of my new investments turned out to be a brand new computer. They were still in their infancy then and not many homes had them.

Clearly it was time to start searching on-line.

I fired up the automatic dial-up modem and waited for the computer to spring into life. Feeling a bit sheepish like a naughty schoolboy, I looked around the room to see that no-one was watching and typed in the words 'fetish footwear'.

This modern piece of technology whirred into action. What a surprise! Thousands of hits, pictures and sites came flooding onto the screen all showing exactly the kind of outrageous clothing and footwear my mysterious new customer was after. Armed with this new information my next move was clear.

Was all the merchandise on-line of the quality that Sue was looking for? Clearly not, otherwise she wouldn't have contacted me. It was as if it was meant to be. Could I have discovered a niche market? Could this be the new direction for W. J. Brookes?

It was important for me to share my new project with my wife, Sara. Would she understand? Of course she would! She'd spent some time as a rep for Ann Summers, the respectable end of titillation who, in the words of their advertisements, 'Have been providing the people of the UK with everything they need for a hot and satisfying sex life for over 40 years'. It was obvious that she'd be a useful resource.

Sara is level headed, extremely intelligent, worldly wise and has a good sense of humour…normally!!

"You're what?" Her riotous laughter could be heard three streets away. "W. J. Brookes, the masters of Brogues and traditional footwear? Making boots for cross-dressers and saucy girlies who are probably all 'on the game'? Now I've heard everything."

"I'm serious. The woman on the phone told me about the demand and the fact that very few people are making them. It seems it's an undersupplied market. So it has to be a no-brainer. Anyway, I can't lose anything by at least doing some research."
"And I suppose that means taking out a year's subscription to these!" She picked up a couple magazines. "Were they any use?"
"Not really, but it was worth looking!!!"

"I bet it was." She chucked them down on the table. "Better not leave these around, don't want Dan getting any ideas. You should be setting an example to your son!" She laughed again. "Actually, if it works it's brilliant."

"Honest? You're seriously OK with this?" I couldn't believe what she was saying.
"Of course. I must get on with dinner." She responded as if this were a regular evening conversation.

She headed off to the kitchen. Did that just happen? It wasn't the reaction I'd expected.

"So what's for dinner tonight?" I said suddenly remembering that I hadn't eaten at lunchtime.
"Chicken." She turned round, pointedly and coquettishly adding, "And, I suppose you'd like breast, leg AND thigh?

I flopped into my chair and tried to fathom out whether her response was genuine or not. Yet another problem to overcome.

But then a cold chill came over me. So far so good, telling Sara was one thing. Then, how was I going to get my loyal, hardworking employees, friends and colleagues to drop their inhibitions and make a range of boots and shoes that were literally two-and-a-half feet of 'sex on legs'?

THAT was my next hurdle.

"A high heeled thigh boot isn't just a kinky boot; it's a journey from one world into another."
Steve Pateman

II

Looking Back to Step Forward!

The next day I had to walk onto the factory floor, gather my workforce together, my friends, my elders and tell them that I was going to do something that would probably give my Father a heart attack and make my Grandfather turn in his grave.

The employees had to be told, but how would they take it from me? They all knew the shoe trade inside out and backwards. Even though I'd taken over from my father who had retired, I was still a young whipper-snapper. How would they take my news?

The easiest way to start was to tell the women in the closing room. This is where all the cut pieces of leather are stitched together to form the top part of the shoe that we call 'the uppers'.

This was on the top floor of our three-storey factory - a place that could reduce the strongest of men to tears if they dared to enter the dragon's den. At Christmas, when the women were in party mood, I've seen the bravest men broken and turned into quivering wrecks if they ventured upstairs, hoping they'd survive the ordeal and make it back down stairs to safety with, hopefully, their trousers still intact!!!!

"You're not serious Steve! Sexy boots? Here? At Brookes's?"
"Yes Vera, sexy boots and shoes." There I'd said it. "What's more, we're going to make them for women AND men."
"Men? Who's gonna buy them then?" An obvious question.
"Well Margaret, drag queens, cross dressers…you know, people in the entertainment business." I said wondering what was next.
"Poofs in boots, then?" They all laughed. "Can we do the measuring for the blokes? All the way up?" The raw, non-politically correct factory humour and raucous laugher had started to kick in.

"And grab a handful while we're at it?" said Gwen digging Margaret in the ribs with her elbow.
"At your age, Gwen?"
"Yer never too old, Maggie!"

I was in danger of causing a mini riot!

"OK, come on, calm down." I shouted above the noise. "Sure, it sounds a bit different, but they are boots and shoes all the same."

I had to defend the decency of the project. "I know it may be a departure from our normal output, but it's something I want us to do."
"What will yer Dad say, Steve?"
"And yer Grandad? What would he have said?"
"Yea." They chorused. "What would they both think?"

Lizzie and Evelyn had worked for W. J. Brookes for years; they'd both worked all through my Dad's leadership and even for a year or two under my Grandad.

When my Dad was running the business he'd taken it forward; he'd been clever at finding new markets and trying many new styles, but nothing as radical as this.

As for Grandad; it's true little had changed in the layout of the factory or the machinery since his day. But my new project would certainly be a shock to the system!

We had no modern communication system, in fact, if Grandad was down on the factory floor and was wanted in the office, they'd ring one blast on the factory hooter. If my Dad was wanted they do it twice and if it was time for a tea-break they did it three times!

Of course, there were no computers. When I arrived straight from school at the tender age of sixteen they were still doing the accounts in ledgers, with a ready reckoner to help them. It really was like something out of a Charles Dickens novel!

But I was in my thirties, Factory Manager and raring to go; keen to update everything in the factory. Intercoms, fax machine, photocopier, new phones; it all had to be done. But something like a range of sexy boots was way beyond modern!

As a teenager, if you had told me that one day I would potentially be making stiletto-heeled, thigh-length red leather boots and that I would be going to fetish shows and cross-dressing events, I would have laughed in your face!

You see, from school all I wanted to do was to join the Royal Marines. Well, that never happened, but I'm now a firefighter, a keen rugby player and supporter of the Northampton Saints. My heart was always set on an exciting, challenging and somewhat dangerous career.

With hindsight I realise that some things do happen for the best. But the last thing I ever wanted to do was to join the family business.

So, from a never-to-be Royal Marine to a firefighter, it's the years in between that have been so important to me. Years that stretched me professionally and opened my mind personally. Years I wouldn't swap for the world. Years that most of all, taught me tolerance and understanding about a way of life I never knew; a way of life that was a zillion light-years away from the world I was brought up in.

Here follows a bit of history, a bit of background to the story. Oh, nothing too heavy, it's just important for you to know.

I was born in Wellingborough in Northamptonshire right in the very heart of England. It was once a thriving boot and shoe town, where there was a shoe factory on almost every corner! Its other great industry, that of iron ore quarrying, employed hundreds of men from the 1860s for the next hundred years.

There was a time when just about every village in this part of Northamptonshire had shoe factories. There were literally dozens of them. They employed men, women and teenagers and just about every family had someone who worked in those noisy, dirty factories. It was a way of life.

In 1889 William Brookes and his brother-in-law, a Mr Austin, built a small factory in King Street on the edge of the village of Earls Barton, midway between Wellingborough and the county town, Northampton. Then in 1906 it was sold to William Cox and my great grandfather, Thomas Pateman.

In Earls Barton, in the nineteenth century, there were around thirty boot and shoe makers working in lean-to sheds or outbuildings attached to the back of their houses.

Then, as machinery was introduced, most of the workers found employment in one of the many factories in the village. Industrialisation had arrived.

However, in the 1930s came The Great Depression and by the mid-1990s there were only five factories left in Earls Barton. Before long there were only two, the famous Barker Shoes and W.J. Brookes. Quite honestly, when you think of the way the rest went to the wall, it was amazing that we survived for so long.

Earls Barton is a lively village with a tight-knit, thriving community. It's set high above the valley of the River Nene and is famous for its magnificent solid Saxon tower that in 1972 featured on a Royal Mail 4p postage stamp!

For some unknown reason the village has always been celebrated for growing leeks (of all things) and for its famous Earls Barton Leek Pie that the older villagers still cook on Shrove Tuesday.

Anyone who's born and bred in the village is called 'a leek', but if you talk to some of the real old 'Bartoners' they'll tell you that to be a real Bartoner you have to have been born in the original old village.
Northamptonshire's factories have been famous for boots and shoes for centuries, even making boots for Oliver Cromwell's Model Army during the seventeenth-century English Civil War.

My Great-grandfather started off by making things like fishermen's waders made out of sealskins, and also Cossack boots for the Russian army. Those Russian's boots were so big at the top of the leg, the soldiers used to stuff straw down them to keep warm in the harsh Russian winters.

With the onslaught of the 1914-18 World War, along with most of the factories in Northamptonshire, we started making boots for the officers and soldiers.

Then, after the end of that Great War, it was back to making traditional boots and shoes. In 1939, yet again our production was interrupted, and we were commandeered by the War Office to make more boots for a new generation of soldiers.

In the mid 1940s, after the war, we tried to get back to the normality of making fine, traditional English shoes that made the county famous the world over: Brogues, Chelsea Boots, Oxfords and Gibsons.

After we said goodbye to the war years we started being involved with completely new clients. Believe it or not, it was the Teddy Boys who partly dictated our new production.

For them we made men's shoes with a high instep and very pointed toes; these were known as 'Winkle Pickers'. The other hugely popular fashion shoe was called the 'Brothel Creeper'; these had crepe soles that were an inch thick. The story goes that these originated just after the war in 1945 when 'our boys' were demobbed from the Forces.

On their way home the soldiers spent time in London, enjoying the freedom they so much deserved. They'd visit the seedy nightspots of King's Cross and Soho and it wasn't long before their crepe-soled desert boots became known as brothel creepers. We, like so many other shoemakers, adapted the style in the 1950s and they became a 'must have' for the Teddy Boys.

As the 50s gave way to the 60s we started making footwear for Shellys Shoes of London and Johnson's of the King's Road; both were famous for being leaders of fashion and were frequented by pop stars as well as the rich and famous.

It was then that we unwittingly entered the world of show-biz. We made the chisel toed, high Cuban heeled, elastic-sided Chelsea boots for an up-and coming group called 'The Beatles'!!!

Then, as fashion took hold in the swinging 60s/early 70s, a new fashion evolved, better known as 'The Glam Rock' era. Our range of boots and shoes of many colours and materials had to be made with the highest possible heels and platforms. One or two of our clients were Mud, Elton John, Alvin Stardust and Gary Glitter to name but a few.

Then in the mid to late 70s came the revolution of Punk music, which gave way to the 80s, the birth of the new electronic-style of music and of more big star customers like Adam Ant and Boy George.

The choice of footwear of the New Romantics of the 80s, such as Duran Duran and Human League, was an all suede pixie style boot with a big fold-down suede cuff. These really reflected the fashions of the day as everyone was wearing puffy white shirts and baggy trousers.

Our biggest customer of the 80s pop scene was The Jam. We made a different pair of shoes for each member of the iconic group and they wore them in the photos that featured on their album covers and also on stage in their touring gigs. Consequently the black shoes with white uppers became big sellers. The Jam were probably one of the last groups whose fans were so loyal they copied the way their heroes dressed and, naturally, the fans had to have the shoes as well.

It was in the 80s that Shellys Shoes, who'd been commissioning us since the 1960s, suggested we should go to the GDS Düsseldorf Shoe Fair; arguably one of the biggest of its kind in the world. My Dad went with me and it really opened our eyes to the competition we faced.

"When I was young," he said as we walked round one of the thirteen vast halls full of exhibitors, "all I had to worry about was the shoe factory in the next village. Now look, it's Earls Barton versus the world! In my day a big trip was a business meeting in London. Now look at us! We're travelling to Düsseldorf for a day! It just shows how much the world has shrunk."

We tried to keep up with fashion, but it was ever-evolving and by the 90s things had changed completely, beyond all our expectations. The 16 to 25-year-olds didn't want to mimic their pop idols any longer and fashion took on the sporty look of Nike, Adidas and Reebok. Everybody had to have famous names prominently advertising their brand logos on their shirts, trousers or footwear. Suddenly the brand name became more important than the style and that's still how it is today.

We even made shoes for international star designers like Joe Casely-Hayford, John Richmond and Vivienne Westwood, as well as making boots for many major feature films such as 'Batman' and 'Tank Girl', in addition to shoes for the stars including Blurr, Oasis, The Spice Girls, David Essex and Lenny Henry.

But the rebellious side of fashion was on our side, competing as it did with 'Grunge'. The footwear mirrored the clothes. Enter a shabby, very casual, industrial style; a hard and very masculine look, generally black with a commando sole and anything from three eyelet shoes to 28 eyelet calf-length boots with steel toe-caps.

The enduring brand leader was Doc Martens worn by everyone from Pop singers to Pope John Paul II. In fact, when His Holiness was presented with a pair of white DMs, he was so impressed with them, that he immediately ordered 100 pairs for his staff.

The 90s also saw an even bigger change to the English shoe industry and that had nothing to do with fashion. It was politics!!!

Small businesses were facing difficult times. As a family firm, we had always lived within our means; we never borrowed money and always watched the balance of our books like hawks. The trouble was that continuing to make the same shoes that we'd been making for years wasn't going to keep us afloat. We needed new markets, new styles and a bigger customer base.

One of the things I wanted to do, much to the consternation of my family, was to make changes; we had to modernise. In my first years in the factory we were turning out between eighty and a hundred pairs of shoes a day and we had about seventy workers on the payroll. By the 1990s we were making ten times more each day, but with a workforce of about eighty.

We were a small business; in years gone by companies like ours were the life-blood of Britain. Is it any surprise that Napoleon called us "A nation of shopkeepers" and to that we must add "small firms".

Mrs Thatcher, under whose leadership so many small firms went to the wall, ought to have known how important this was. After all her father had a small business as an independent grocer in Grantham, even though he and his forebears started life as boot and shoe workers in Ringstead and Raunds, not far from Earls Barton in Northamptonshire.

Then came John Major. With him the value of the pound went up prior to the General Election. In time our international customers started to freeze their orders. They were understandably cautious and reluctant to continue ordering from us, and others, with such an expensive pound.

Orders were cancelled or held and we had to put our workers on short time. It was something that we'd never done before and it had a dramatic effect on my Father and me. Every part of the factory had hundreds of boxes full of shoes, awaiting 'call-in' from our foreign buyers.

My Dad was hoping to retire in the late 1990s and I was being trained to take over. This was hardly the time to be experimenting with outrageous new lines, but needs must when the Devil drives!

Little did I know then that boots and shoes would take me to a world of gay clubs, fetish clubs and swinger's clubs, meeting with cross dressers, drag queens and the world of erotica!

And that brings me back to the story! With quite a bit of research under my belt, the dream had to become a reality. Initially three things were essential; I needed someone to help me with the designs; I had to convince the workforce that I wasn't cracking up; and most of all, I needed some sexy legs to model the samples.

I was sure one of the girls in the factory might offer to model the women's samples. There was no problem there. But, Heaven help me, what about the men's? For the first time in my life I had to admit I was desperate…I needed a bloke in stiletto heels!

It looked as though, just possibly, Earls Barton could turn Kinky!!!

"Often I am asked if I regret getting into kinky boots. The only regret I have is not doing it sooner!! But then timing is everything!"
Steve Pateman

III

It's All in The Legs!

"Who'd like to earn fifty quid, cash in hand?"

The response from the women had been amazingly positive. The jokes flowed, the innuendos, the laughter and the thought of getting their hands on some really sexy footwear; they loved the idea. When I asked for a fitting model to try the boots and shoes on I had no shortage of volunteers, it seemed as though the cash incentive wasn't important.

Of the women who'd offered to model, Bev struck me as the one with the figure and legs that would be perfect for getting the designs from the drawing board to production.

The men, however, were another matter as I ventured down into the lasting and making room. This is the heart of the factory where the shoes are fully assembled, where the 'upper' from the closing room meets the sole. This is the first time the separate components come together to actually look like a shoe.

When it was time to confront them with my proposal, they stood, or leaned on their machines, with arms folded as if to say, "Go on, thrill us with your next mad idea!" It was the first stage of me revealing my new project to the men. I offered the same cash incentive to the men as I had to the women.

"What've we got to do for it?" shouted one of the workers. Such enthusiasm! How long that would last?
"I need someone to model. Basically, I need a complete set of feet and legs that we can base some new patterns on." I said, trying to keep it humorous and light.

A couple of hands belonging to more senior members of my staff came down, but most of them stayed up, waving, like school-kids wanting to be chosen for an errand.

"It's a new and exciting range. Something very different. I need a bloke," I added sheepishly almost under my breath, "to do the modelling for me."

A few more arms and spirits weakened and disappeared. Then Bert stood up from behind his machine.

"Great," I said, "thank you Bert, you won't be sorry."

"Now, 'ang on a minute," he barked in his usual grumbling way. "I ain't offerin'."

His reaction didn't surprise me; in fact I knew there was no way he'd do it. He was the Alpha Male of the 'lasting and making' rooms. To him anything less masculine than a 'bovver boot' was for wimps and cissies. Then it dawned on me, his wife worked upstairs, and she'd obviously had her ear to the ground and heard the rumours I was planning a sexy new range.

"Is this all about them boots, the kinky ones?" Bert said.

"Y…E…S," I drawled, steeling myself for the onslaught.

I'm the boss, I told myself, be strong.

"Is there a problem Bert?"
"Well, I for one ain't doin' it, and I reckon I speak for 'em all 'ere." Bert said, slowly rotating his head, staring at the last few of the raised hands.

One by one, as the men looked at each other and then at Bert, some of the hands slowly sank into the security of their pockets while others were left with their arms crossed tightly over their leather aprons.

"Surely one of you blokes?" I appealed, not very optimistically. "Craig? Barry? No-one's going to see you, well, only from thighs down. It's fifty quid. It's money for old rope."
"It may be 'old rope' to you Steve," Bert sneered, "but some of us ain't that desperate."
"Why don't you ring Lily Savage?" a joker from the back shouted.
"Or Danny la Rue!" quipped another voice that obviously had an inkling of what it was all about.
"Or," growled Bert (of course, he'd want the last word)… "It's your bloody idea. Why don't you do it?"

Raucous laughter echoed around the room. Slowly men and machines became united. One or two of them had grasped what it was all about and, with one hand on the hip and blowing imaginary kisses to each other, they minced back to their machines.

OK, round one to them. But I wasn't going to let it rest. At least I'd got the women on my side. Now back to the men!! Could I still rally them to the cause??

"All right, so maybe you're all too shy. Perhaps you're too ashamed of your varicose veins or your knobbly knees. But I'll find someone, don't worry.

27

These 'Kinky Boots' as you call them are going to be made and someone's going to model them. And this could be the salvation of this factory."

It's not often the cloud of depression descends on me, but I didn't know whether I was sinking fast or just temporarily deflated. Probably both. It wasn't until I got home that night and told my tale of woe to Sara that things became obvious to both of us.

"It's got to be you, Steve!" Sara had the biggest grin on her face since I don't know when. "Do it. Why not?"
"Because if I do, they've won."
"Don't be daft." Sara was nothing if not practical, supportive and…usually right. "They were only doing what, deep down, you knew they'd do. I mean, can you imagine Ernie or Dez doing it; or Bert? Come on get real. It's your project, you do it. You know the look, the style and what you want to achieve. It has to be you."

I knew she was right; I hated having to admit it. It was my project, my dream, and more than that, it was a possible lifeline for the business. If anyone was going to make a bloody fool of himself in a 'do or die situation', it had to be me. As my old man would say, "Lead by example", but was this one step too far?

My legs weren't all that bad and I am shoe size eleven, a good reasonably average fitting. I could be good for the job but at the back of my mind there was still that niggling feeling that bosses tend not to do this kind of thing.

So now we had to solve some of the practical problems facing us and my innocent workforce. Fitting boots isn't as straightforward as it might at first seem. There are different leg shapes for a start. And although it sounds obvious, men's legs are different from women's.

We had to do more research, this time practical research. We had to talk legs! Measure them!!! Study them!!!! Jenny and Joey my designers, who were just as enthusiastic as I was, were willing to help in doing the measuring.

Jenny went and measured the women's and I did the unenviable task of measuring the men's legs; well, those who were up for it! We had to relate the size of the foot to the height of the person. We made a list of measurements, their build, ankle, calf, mid-calf, top of calf, knee height, knee and carefully, the thigh measurements! The results were staggering.

"I never realised there was such a difference." Jenny studied the vital statistics we'd gathered. "Vera's six feet tall yet her leg measurements are the same as Olive's and she's only five feet six."

I looked at Jenny's list. "And the men's calves are in a totally different position from the women's." I'd been in the shoe trade for quite a while, but all this had never really occurred to me.

"Well", I said, "we can do a range for both. Women's from threes to sevens and men's from sevens to thirteens."

We looked at each other and both got insanely excited. Ideas started flowing, each getting worse and worse and sillier and sillier as we continued to brainstorm. However, the possibilities and crazy designs plus the look were slowly coming alive. We soon realised that in this new project the only restrictions or limitations were in our minds. Suddenly the idea of getting Lily Savage wasn't so crazy after all.

Women's boots and shoes were a new area for us. W.J. Brookes, like all of Northamptonshire's boot and shoe manufactures, had always concentrated on men's footwear whereas ladies' shoes were mostly made in Leicester or Norwich.

But we had some facts and those facts spoke volumes, and they spoke very loudly; in fact they shouted at the top of their voices: "Steve, you could become the King of Kinky Boots for women and men."

I was getting really excited about the new venture and gradually as the workers, male and female, slowly accepted my idea, they all started to share my excitement…or were they just better actors than I thought?

The next step was to get a sample made. Something basic to get on with. I gave a pair of my Oxford Brogues to a last maker in Northampton. The last is a plastic block shaped like a shoe. The leather 'upper' is stretched over it to give the final appearance of a shoe. It is then that it moves on to another department to have the sole fitted.

"Look Mike, you know lasts inside out. This is a good honest bespoke man's shoe, can you remake it into a last for high heels so that it would feel comfy as a made-to-measure when I put it on?"

A bit of head scratching from Mike. "I don't see why not. A wider fit, alter the pitch and standardize the heel and you're good to go." He was so practical, as though I had asked him to just knock up an ordinary men's last. We were on our way. Once we had the new last I called in our insole makers explaining what I was planning to achieve.

The first consideration was that the boot or shoe had to stand a great deal of weight if men were going to wear them. That meant we'd have to reinforce the insole; that's the foundation of any high-heeled footwear. We realised that a shaped metal plate had to be inserted into the arch of the shoe to support the foot.

Then critically, the stiletto heel needed a heavier grade stainless steel rod moulded into the plastic of the heel in order to support the weight of an eighteen stone man in full drag and make-up!!

The next stage was to get patterns made for some test samples. Luckily enough, one of our customers, Joey, a pattern maker and designer in Leicester, offered to help us get going. He had made and designed many styles for men and women in the past, as well as boots and shoes in men's and women's sizes. Not only that, but he had also designed a lot of footwear with high heels, platform soles, zips up the side. He'd worked with black and red PVC; all rather sexy I thought. He knew all the tricks of the trade especially as PVC is harder to work with than leather, so his help was going to be invaluable.

The International Footwear Fair in Düsseldorf was fast approaching. It was held twice a year in March and September. Could we make a small collection, perhaps two or three variations, to show there? There were thirteen vast halls at the exhibition centre and all the Northamptonshire shoemakers were in one section of one of those halls. Once again we'd feel like minnows in a shark-infested sea, but we had to go for it. We had to see if there was a market for the boots.

So we booked a stand. It was 25 square metres on which we had to show our usual range of high quality, typically English footwear, our fashion styles, creepers, winkle pickers, our heavy grunge fashion boots, but right in the centre of our stand, were our new samples in a prominent position. I had designated a small space for our new range, 'The Boots'. Yes, you've guessed; in red, black, leather, patent and PVC, they stood out like beacons on a dark night!

No one in those vast halls was showing anything like our new range. They were something of a talking point and certainly entertaining. As people visited our stand I was amazed; to most people they seemed to mesmerise and awaken a forgotten animal urge. They touched them, felt them, fondled them, stroked them, and it was then, for the first time, I saw these boots and shoes in a new light.

I began to realise that these weren't just items of footwear; they were coming alive. They had their own personality. They were kicking open doors, unlocking secret fantasies; they were central to a new way of life.

Suddenly I knew my creation could change lives, including mine, forever.

"High-heeled shoes and boots are the master key to all our fantasies; they can unlock our most secret desires and dreams."
Steve Pateman

IV

The Seal of Approval

"What? How much? Are you out of your mind? Is this company on a suicide mission?"

I had a sneaky feeling Dad wasn't impressed with my latest suggestion!

When we got back from Düsseldorf the time seemed right to get my Dad, who was the Chairman of the Board of Directors, on my side. I had already mentioned we had a new line, but not in any detail. In fact, he had no idea what was up my sleeve. This was going to be tough, and furthermore, the bit I most dreaded telling him was that we needed to make an investment in the project. A big one.

I started to tell him about the new range, making ladies' style shoes in men's sizes: sevens to thirteens. A look of total confusion came across his face, as though I was quoting the quantum laws of physics.

"High heeled boots for men? What, like waders?"
"No Dad, not quite." Well there's a thought! "No they're for the erotic fashion market."
"Well there ain't much that's erotic about waders."

I was losing the will to live.

"Dad, they're sexy high-heeled boots for men. They're for cross dressers"

"What are they cross about?" Innocence! If it wasn't so serious I'd laugh.
"No Dad, they're men who dress up as women. Come on you've heard of drag queens, haven't you? What about the dames in pantomime?"
"Ah, I know what you mean now, like Les Dawson?"

A light seemed to flicker a little.

"Sort of, Dad," I wasn't really winning this round. I thought,
"Just agree, let's move on". At this point I went for it. I pulled out some photos and put them down in front of him and expected him to be shocked.
"Oh, you mean like in the sixties? Why didn't you say? You could have saved us all some time."

I pulled the photos away from him; they were too much of a distraction.

"So…let me get this right." Dad leaned back in his chair, "You want to buy a machine that attaches ladies high heels to men's shoes and boots?"

Bull's eye!

Making boots and shoes is a complicated business. What we had to do was a totally different process from how we normally attach our heels. We'd done exhaustive tests on the weight-bearing qualities of our new, improved stilettos and were satisfied they'd hold the heaviest of drag queens!

All our machinery was geared to our regular output and every time we created a new design there were small changes to be made to our equipment. But this was a major change and a major gamble.

We needed the new machine. It was going to cost £16,000 and there was bound to be more outlay to come on patterns, materials and production time.

"Yes, I've already contacted the British United Shoe Machinery Company and they've got me one on trial and if it all goes well, we can buy it at a reduced rate of £16,000."
"£16 grand! You call that reduced?"
"I'm certain the gamble will pay off." I started to tell Dad about Düsseldorf.
"Honest Dad, I wish you could have been there, the reaction was incredible. I never dreamed the interest would be so great."
"What about orders?" Was that all that really mattered to Dad?
"I'll come to that in a minute. It's obvious the market is really wide and if we can capture the market who knows what could happen?"
"What about orders?"

"Dad, if they'd been in production, we'd have taken hundreds of orders, that's how great the interest was. There are twenty shops across Europe and the UK that are desperate for these boots and shoes, but because it was our new range they want to see some samples first."

I was preparing to play my ace card, "You see Dad, with the interest we had in Düsseldorf and with the thought that we could corner the niche market, even world-wide…" Here goes! "…there's every possibility this new venture could actually keep the company going and save W. J. Brookes."

Silence. I knew saving the factory had hit home!

I looked into those eyes; I could almost hear the mind whirring, the cogs clicking into gear, the rubbing of the chin and the pulling of the ear lobes, the usual signs of serious thought. He was starting to see the possibilities.

My hands clasped and unclasped, sweating with anticipation, awaiting approval. Then after what seemed ages, the Oracle spoke.
"You realise that once this money is spent you're committed?"
"I know."
"No turning back?"
"I know."
"This sixteen-thousand-plus quid could be yours; you have nothing to prove."
"I know." That's all I could say.
"Well, if you're sure," Yes, go on, Dad, come out with it, yes or no? "If you're sure, I will back you."
"Thanks Dad, that's brilliant!"

The relief was immense! What he didn't know was the contract for the heel-attaching machine was ready to sign and the machine was already in the factory on a trial basis, ready to make the samples.

Soon after we'd returned from Germany I was asked to do an interview for The Financial Times on behalf of the British Footwear Federation. Around this time the Footwear Federation and the Clothing Federation had amalgamated. Even one of the flagships of British clothing, Marks and Spencer, one of the last remaining supporters of British manufacturers, had to start manufacturing abroad in order to compete in the home market. A strong pound made importing goods cheaper and at the same time for those, like ourselves, it made our products more expensive to export for our foreign customers.

The FT was doing an article about the plight of both the shoe industry and the clothing industry. The effect of the exchange rate was devastating on British manufacturers and wholesalers whose market was mainly abroad. Of our total production round about 90% either directly or indirectly was exported. Even a slight fluctuation in the exchange rate was disastrous for potential orders or orders awaiting despatch.

In my contribution to the article I rather rashly came clean on everything that was occupying my mind at the time. I said that we, one of the most traditional of shoe manufactures, were launching a new range of Kinky Boots and erotic wear, and what's more I made it clear that this was, as I'd said a million times, "make or break time" for W. J. Brookes.

I even went as far as saying that if things didn't look up by Christmas, then it was curtains for the company. I played on our history and told them that after a hundred and fifteen years we might have to make nearly a hundred people join the dole queue, not to mention the knock-on effect on all our suppliers and the local community. I laid it on a bit thick!

Next day, on the way to work, I went to the shop and bought the FT along with my usual paper. I read the article and showed it to the office staff.

"Ooo, you're a celebrity, getting your name in the paper. W. J. Brookes will be famous." Clarice thought this was a real feather in
the cap! She cut the article out and pinned it to the board downstairs on the factory floor. She didn't realise how prophetic her words were at the time.

But soon we were all going to find out.

"Sexy shoes are lingerie for the feet."
Steve Pateman

V

Trouble at the Top

Once again, Rosie buzzed through to me.
"There's a woman on the 'phone."
"A real one?"
"Oh yes, no doubt about it this time!"
"Put her through. And Rosie…?"
"Yes?"
"White and two sugars, please."
"You're on."

On the line was Michele Kurland, an Assistant Producer from the BBC. She said they were filming in the North of England and happened to spot the article in The Financial Times. They were working on a series called 'Trouble at the Top' investigating small companies that were struggling.

"Are you a company that's struggling?"

I could have said all sorts of things like, "What's that got to do with you? How dare you! Get lost!" Instead I simply said, "Yes".
"Oh. Brilliant. Are you really struggling?"
"You have no idea."
The elation of Düsseldorf had slightly worn off. I was beginning to get cold feet about our real situation all over again.

"If we don't get things sorted by Christmas," I said, "there's every possibility that we'll have to close down and make our staff redundant."
"Please don't think I'm being insensitive, but that's brilliant. I mean, it's just the kind of thing we want to feature in the series."

"Really?"

"Yes. As I said, we are soon to start filming for a second series of a programme called 'Trouble at the Top' for BBC2 and we're following companies that are going through rough times and are trying new ways of turning things round."

"Sounds painfully familiar" I chipped in.
"If it's OK with you, we'd like to meet up with you and maybe follow the progress of your 'Kinky Boots' project."

They'd just finished filming with a firm up in the North and they wanted to call in next day on their way back to London. My first thought was, "What have I got to lose?" Then again, reality kicked in. How would Dad and the family react? And what about our employees? If we pulled it off it would be great advertising; on the other hand, if it didn't it could make us look ridiculous.

Next morning the BBC crew turned up. I'd expected King Street to be full of trucks and vans covered with aerials and with 'BBC' splashed all over them. Instead, the main crew had travelled back to base while the producer, Sue, and her Assistant Producer, Michele, came to meet us at the factory.

They were both really nice. They were professional, of course, and gently persuasive and very interested in everything they saw. They looked round and chatted about everything to each other like keen kids on a school outing. As we toured the factory they took a few photos of the machines and the 'stars' - The Boots! I couldn't keep anything from the staff, so I'd pre-warned them first thing and asked them to carry on as normal.

We ended up in the Board Room. Sue was really taken with the fading sepia photos of my predecessors that lined the walls.

She asked me if I'd heard of 'Trouble at the Top"; I had to admit I hadn't. My only experience of reality shows was the 'fly on the wall' type of documentaries when they follow the staff round a hotel somewhere in the North of England.

"Well," Michele said, "similar, but we are more of a business programme. We'd like to follow you through all the processes of making the Kinky Boots, the production and the marketing right through to launching the product in Düsseldorf. This has all the elements of a terrific programme, Mr Pateman." She said, grabbing another biscuit. "It's completely new territory for us and totally different from anything we've featured before or have planned for this series."

"I can see that," I said hesitantly, "but how's that going to affect us? How do you work with these 'spy on the wall' cameras?"

"It's not that type of documentary." She said, "Everything we'll do will be on film; you'll know exactly what's happening as it happens. We'll turn up and do a day's filming here or wherever. It will all be pre-planned. At no point will it be a 'secret spy camera' prying into anything without your full consent, catching people doing things they shouldn't or showing problems with the factory."

"OK, I'm happy with that." Suddenly my reply made her relax visibly.

"You know, Steve, it's all right if I call you Steve?" She knew how to win a chap over. "It could be fabulous. There's scope for some great location filming."
"How do you mean? Round the factory and the village?"

"Oh yes on location and definitely in the factory, it's the Kinky Boots bit that's the real audience catcher. We could get some of the customers being fitted perhaps here, then wearing the boots in the clubs in London, in shows and on stage. What do you think? The guys, mainly the drag queens and the cross-dressers, would really make the programme. That would really make it stand out."

"I can see it would be something a bit different." I said.
"I'll say," she spluttered, almost choking on her coffee, "it could be sensational."

There was one question that had to be asked even though I didn't really want to. "How much will you be paying us for this?"
"Er no, sorry. We are the BBC and we don't pay, but think of the excitement and a few meals on expenses. Does that change the possibilities?"
"No, but what's in it for me?"
"Publicity, Steve, publicity."

Appealing, I thought. Once I got over the shock of not being paid thousands and retiring to the Bahamas, it would certainly bring welcome publicity; after all millions watch the telly and that couldn't be bad.

The idea and the possibilities were really starting to appeal to me, What could we lose? I had to sell it to the staff; but would they enjoy being part of something like this? Then there was the family. I had to talk to Sara, but I was pretty sure she'd be OK with it. And once again, there was Dad! Would he consider this yet another step too far? It's one thing making thigh boots, but to show them off in front of cameras and for the BBC? That's something else.

"You're a bloody idiot, man," Dad said.

Perhaps I should have told him in a more roundabout way, but how? He carried on making me feel like the naughty boy who'd just hit another cricket ball through the greenhouse windows.

"What happens if it all goes against you? You could look a right fool and what about everyone else? Have you thought about anyone except yourself? Good God, what would my Father say, tarting round on the telly selling your porno boots?"

"Dad." I appealed.
"Go on, do it. But don't forget what I think; don't touch it with a barge pole."

I knew he was right, but still I was convinced that if I could pull it off, it could be good news for the factory. This was something I really had to do.

"Oh come on, it's all about Brookes. It's our story about our struggle, our survival. The BBC producers have promised that I'm going to be in control. It's going to be a history about the factory, a programme about the people. Just think, in the future we'll be able to look back and see how a factory like ours worked and survived. It'll be a great thing for W. J. Brookes, a video record of our efforts to save the company."

Well, that was part of my reason; the other thing was, since I wasn't getting paid for it, how else could we get the company known to such a wide audience? If we were to go on television we could instantly be known for our footwear, for our Kinky Boots. So as much as they were using me for a free programme, I was going to use them for free advertising, the sort my new project could never afford, and definitely could not get in any other way.

There was yet another of those rather long silences. "Well, we'll see what comes of it in a few years," Dad sad, "if you've really made your mind up to go for it, OK, I'll back you. I'm just warning you, that's all."

"You won't regret it, I promise." I said, desperately trying not to let my own doubts rise to the surface.
"Regret? I've nothing to regret, let's hope you haven't in the future."

Thanks Dad. That made me feel even worse!

So I made the call to Michele and agreed to do it. It was a time to think positively. If I could only pull it off.

"I'm so pleased!" said the voice the other end in perfect BBC English, "would you like me to send some videos of previous programmes, just to give you some idea of the kind of things we expect of you?"

Since I'd never seen any of the series before, that would be a real help. I could watch them, make notes about what I'd do and what I wouldn't, what I liked and what I hated, what I'd allow them to do and what I'd veto. My mind was racing wildly again; after all, they were coming into my world, my factory and an industry that they knew little about, but which was my territory. What could possibly go wrong?

It was like the feeling you get when you're on a roller-coaster. They lock you in, the barrier comes down, you jerk into action then you slowly climb up, up, up; knowing that any moment, you'll be hurtling down, down, down into…the unknown.

"Designing a sexy pair of boots has not only got to be practical but also to give the impression of being totally impractical to wear."
Steve Pateman

VI

Lights, Camera, Action!

With Dad on my side, very soon a second meeting was arranged which was when I laid down the rules. It was a difficult situation because once the programme had been made, they'd just walk away and start on another show, but people in the village and especially my employees would have to live with whatever had been put into that programme and that would stay with the village for ever. I wanted it to be dead right and hopefully something that would be of benefit to us and to the community.

"Look I'm not getting paid for it. You'll be on my turf, I want you to treat me and my workforce with respect and decency. We don't want anything out of the blue, no surprises. I don't want you manufacturing things that don't happen or making anyone look stupid, especially me and my family."
"Yes, yes, we can do that. We won't surprise you"
"What about the editing?" This was something else that concerned me.

At the back of my mind was something from years ago. As a teenager I was in our local church Youth Club and it was led by an actor called Arnold Peters. He had played Jack Woolley, one of the lead characters in The Archers on BBC Radio 4 for years; in fact he'd been in the radio soap almost since it began back in the 1950s. He had also played loads of parts in sit-coms like 'Last of the Summer Wine', 'Only Fools and Horses' and 'Dad's Army'.

Two or three times he arranged for us all to go to London to watch live recordings of BBC TV shows. On one memorable occasion Arnold took us to watch the filming of 'Citizen Smith' starring Robert Lindsay and what was most brilliant was that we went back stage afterwards and had a long chat with him. At that time he was one of the biggest names on TV and everyone was going round using his Wolfie catch phrase, "Power to the People".

A lot of what we saw being filmed never ended up in the finished programme, and if that happened with 'Trouble at the Top', it could influence how it came over to the viewer. Indiscriminate editing could distort what was said.

"What about my right of editorial control." I asked rather bravely. "How involved will I be? Do I have a say in it? What if you distort the facts too much?"

"You have no right over editorial control." came the frank and uncompromising reply.

Well, that took the wind out of my sails. It was a huge stumbling block.

"Having said that, you will be involved at every stage, I promise you. It's not in our interest to do anything but tell your story the way it is. And if, after we've edited it, there's something you really are unhappy with, then we'll reconsider and possibly even re-film it."

That softened the blow a bit.

"It's your story. You'll be feeding us the facts and you'll be with us all the way while we're filming."

"What about identifying people. Some of them might not want to be named or even shown." I had to ask this, it was important.

"Steve, we are the BBC. We have guidelines, we do everything we can to protect everyone involved and we never name or even show people who want to stay anonymous."

I'd accepted the fact about no editorial control and so, quite honestly, there was no reason not to say yes. When I did, they were obviously delighted.

There were to be six programmes being broadcast in the new series and we were going to be around the third or fourth in the run. Number one programme was going to be their shining light to kick the series off. It featured the launching of Vogue magazine in Russia. That was going to be their big pull; the headliner for them.

I was happy with that. After all, we knew our story was hardly comparable with Vogue Magazine getting into Russia!

Then came the nitty-gritty. They were coming in half-way through our story. We'd already designed and made prototypes, we'd been to Düsseldorf, so we'd have to turn the clock back and re-enact some of the early parts of the story.

This was really going to be tricky because once you've already done something, if you're not a real actor, it's hard to fake the surprise or the way you felt at certain times. But, as you'll see, it all worked out and they were happy with our dubious acting skills!!

They decided that on the first day of filming they wanted to do some background shots around the factory and village. They suggested a date. Oh dear, that was the first problem!!

"Sorry," I felt awful saying this at their first attempt at getting things going, "I've an appointment to go to London to see a new customer. He's interested in possibly taking the Kinky Boots on."

The customer was one of the new leads from the first Düsseldorf show and I couldn't let this pass. He ran a big warehouse in London specialising in everything to do with the 'adult entertainment' industry. I was thinking that the producers would be annoyed, but instead...

"Oh that's fantastic, we'll film it." That wasn't what I expected.

"Look, I don't know this guy very well, we only met briefly in Düsseldorf. Hopefully, he would become a brand new customer, perhaps it wouldn't be such a good idea."
"Well, why don't you give him a ring?"

"I don't know about that. It's a bit of an imposition, we haven't seen him since the show." But they weren't going to give up that easily.

"Well, we'll ring him."
"No you bloody well won't! This is my customer. What about a compromise? Look, I'll ring him up and tell him about the programme and the BBC. If he's happy, then I'll go with it." Rather nervously I dialled his number.

I didn't expect for one moment that he'd agree because a lot of these companies are a bit secretive and protective of themselves and their customers.

"Oh, that's no problem," he said, "I deal with these people all the time, we've always got the cameras in here doing various stories."
"Are you serious?" I was completely blown away.
"Yea, yea, bring 'em along, no probs."

That was a surprise. Thinking about how it would go, I needed to get things sorted with this guy just in case it didn't work out. What if they filmed something embarrassing? Luckily I was in the office so I could talk to him out of ear-shot of the BBC guys.

"Well, thanks for agreeing, but look, just in case you're not interested, can we have a sort of code-word or phrase, so they don't film something that could be an embarrassing moment for me? Then if you don't want to buy anything it will still look OK."
"Sure that's fine. What d'you have in mind?"

"Well, if you're not interested say something like, "Steve, I love your designs, but we've got our current catalogue printed and ready to come out soon, why don't we wait until we're preparing the next one?"

So we agreed that's what we'd do. I thought poor bloke, the first time we have a proper meeting with him and I put him through this. So I went back to the production team and told them he's happy to do it to camera, but they would have to be careful and sensitive to his customers and staff. They agreed.

The day of filming approached. There are times when you look back on events that you regret. This was definitely one of those. The night before filming I went out to a Round Table meeting with the lads and as usual we had a few drinks and ended up at the local curry house. This was probably not the best thing to have done with a big appointment in London early the next day.

Next morning Sara dropped me off at Wellingborough station. I usually stood all the way with everybody else at rush hour, but this was to be a real treat. The BBC told me which train to catch to St Pancras. They had paid for me to travel in style and even booked me a reserved seat.

I'd recently bought my first mobile phone and I had a big suitcase full of samples and my rucksack; I felt very special! The case had a handle and two squeaky wheels that became almost my trademark in 'Trouble at the Top'; they would film me so often lugging it round the streets of London that those squeaky wheels became almost as recognisable as me.

Halfway to London they phoned, "Just to say everything's all set up; we're waiting for you at the bottom of St Pancras Station for your arrival."

I hadn't bargained for this, "What do you mean, all set up?"
"Oh don't worry, we're just going to do a bit filming of you arriving in London"

"OK," I said wondering what else they'd got up their BBC sleeves. This was the first time they had sprung something on me and it certainly wouldn't be the last! "What do you want me to do?"
"Just relax and enjoy the journey, we'll ring you again just before the train gets in and we'll explain then."

Relax? Hello? Suddenly the butterflies started doing a marathon round my inner circle, stirring up last night's curry!

Sure enough, ten minutes before arrival my mobile rang again. "OK, what do you want me to do?" I was suddenly aware of other passengers' eavesdropping.

"Stay on the train and let the commuter rush go first," Michele was now very business like, "then get off the train and walk straight down the platform. Don't take any notice of anything you see at the end of the platform and when you get to the barrier I want you to turn right towards the ticket office and make your way out towards the taxis."

Then sweaty palms, together with the clenching and unclenching of my fingers, joined the butterflies. The train came to a standstill. It was just past rush-hour. People were jumping up and getting ready to get off. They were pushing and struggling to get to the doors and there I was, sitting like Billy-no-mates as the train started to empty, mobile in hand, waiting to be told my fate.

The phone rang. "Action!"

"OK." I tried to act normally.

Little boy lost, up from the country, coming to the big city; it was then that I realised how long the platform was at St Pancras. There were still loads of people walking along and, as we got nearer to the barrier, I could hear the Chinese whispers starting; "There's a camera crew." "What's happening?" "There must be someone famous on the train."

I was thinking, "Bloody hell, here we go." Then the extrovert in me took over and as I drew nearer to the barrier I started to swagger and strut, dangerously being over confident and trying to hide my real feelings. The sweating worsened, but I did what they'd said; I walked past them and headed off to the right towards where the taxis were.

Soon afterwards one of the producers ran up to me and said, "Steve, that was absolutely fantastic. Brilliant. Good job." And that was the point when I knew it was a complete cock-up. They were being polite, what they really meant was "That was bloody awful, we'll have to do it again."

So we did. Back we went to the barrier where a large crowd had now gathered, 'rubber necking' to see who was being filmed. They were all pointing and looking, making me even more nervous. I bet they were saying, "Come on, let's go; it's no one famous."

A minute later one of the sound-men said, "Steve, we're going to wire you for sound; we'll put a microphone on you." This was where the BBC, for the first time, revealed they had no shame! All of a sudden I was stripped there on the platform. They were pulling my shirt out of my trousers; someone had his hand down the back of my shirt; microphones were wired up and clipped behind my tie and a battery pack was fixed to my belt.

"OK Steve, I'm your sound-man. From now on the mic will be live, but if you need to do anything or go anywhere, just tell me and we'll turn it off. By the way, this gear is very expensive, so be careful!"

Then the real filming started. They marched me back up the platform and onto the train again. They put me back in my seat and filmed me from the outside in, then they filmed me from the inside out. They filmed me getting up and down the steps. Time and time again. For the next half an hour I was getting on and off that bloody train!

They eventually agreed that the train sequences were good enough, which was a complete waste of time because that bit never made it to the finished programme. Anyway, we went towards the taxis and I said, "But I don't go by taxi, I always go by tube."

"Ah, we can't film on the tube for technical reasons, so we'll have go by taxi. We've got one booked for the whole day. OK?"

They must have spotted my shocked, worried expression, "Don't worry, the cab's on the Beeb." I thought to myself, too bloody right; it's going to cost an arm and a leg!

"But it's not what I do" I blurted, "when I come to London for a sales pitch it has to be on a budget; people know that on a budget you don't use taxis."

We know that some of the big boys go everywhere by cab, but not me. Still if that's what they wanted, why would I make a fuss!

Anyway, we headed off to the East End. At least that's what I thought. It soon hit me that we were heading in totally the opposite direction. The next thing I knew we were driving past Buckingham Palace, round Victoria and over to Westminster. They must have sensed my questioning looks.

"We're doing this for visuals, we've still got to make it look good to the viewer." OK with me if they wanted to show off some of London's landmarks just to add the glamour.

At last we arrived in the East End and we went in to meet David, the guy I'd spoken to on the phone. He was nice and we had a really good meeting; after a while I forgot about the cameras because it was just like a normal sales pitch.

I was waiting for the 'secret key phrase' to come out. It didn't, so I said, "What d'you think?"

"I like them; I like them a lot," he said to my utter surprise. "But what I really want is leopard skin material in thigh-length boots and court shoes with stiletto heels."

Imagine how I felt. I was blown away, my first-ever sales pitch with the camera running and it was a winner and it wasn't staged! I'd got a real-life customer wanting to buy my Kinky Boots. Wow!

After that we did a couple more sales pitches in the East End and then, true to form, they said it was time for lunch. We went to a restaurant where they insisted on doing some more filming. They wanted my thoughts and reactions about how the meeting had gone.

After such a full-on day I was really, really tired; the beer and curry from my night out were kicking in. The adrenaline had faded and I wanted five minutes of quiet away from them all. So as they started discussing technical details I slunk away from the table and went to the loo for a well-earned break and to gather my thoughts!

Nature took over! The curry was starting to give me a bit of gip. The excitement and the stress were getting at me. I decided that, actually I did want to go to the loo…for real...and quickly.

So to put it politely, I dropped my trousers, sat down and that's when I suddenly remembered the battery pack. Eight hundred quid's worth of high-tech BBC equipment! The sound-man's words rang in my ear, "Don't lose it, don't drop it, be careful with it."

Now picture this. There's me with my trousers down; "Where's the microphone?" Thankfully safe, it was clipped to my tie. I felt around for the battery pack. I must have knocked it in my rush, suddenly it detached itself from my belt and went flying. Thank God I caught it as it fell an inch from the pan. I let out what must have been an ear-splitting 'OH SHIT!"

Visions of me fishing the battery pack out of the bowl and having to disinfect it flooded my brain. Would it ever have worked again? Would I have had to pay for it? Would they sack me? All the sorts of questions that go through your mind at times like that. Anyway, thankfully, it was safe.

I did what I had to do, smartened up and went back to the table rather sheepishly hoping that nobody had spotted my absence. I sat down again with the sound-man right beside me.

He leaned close to me and whispered, "Sounds like you had a good night last night. Don't you remember I did tell you that if you went to the loo, tell me and I'd turn your mic off. I've got all of that on tape."

I blushed scarlet, "You're joking, right?" He winked and laughed, "I'm just glad my mic and battery pack are safe and don't need to go in for decontamination!"

That was my first day's filming. It had been a success; they were happy and I was happy. Kinky Boots had kicked in. The next stage was to arrange for filming back in Earls Barton. They wanted to film different processes. They asked me to get a Rep in, talk to the last maker and generally make plans for the rest of the programme.

"When?" I asked.

"When can you get everyone together? If we come up, we need to be able to do a whole day's filming. We can't come all the way to Earls Barton with a director, producer, assistant producer, lighting, sound, boom operator and so on and hope it just happens; it's got to be planned."

So now, as well as being the star turn, I was to organise the whole day's shooting from my end. A date was set. I'd arranged for everything to happen.

Everyone who should be there was there, nothing could go wrong. We re-enacted all the various processes in the making of the boots and shoes. We had a Rep in to talk about how we selected the leather. We explained all about the fitting and the designs and stressed the important parts, like strengthening the heels and the shank in the insoles so that all the parts of the men's boots were really strong enough to support the weight of a big bloke.

In fact, they followed the making of the sample boots all the way through. My workforce came up trumps! I was conscious that it was disruptive for them, something they don't like doing because it upsets the production run.

Samples are very time consuming and costly both to the employees and to the factory as machine settings have to be altered with valuable time wasted on just one pair. And with the BBC getting in the way it took even longer.

One of the most difficult processes is what we call 'lasting'. It's always quite a challenge. If anything's likely to go wrong it'll be then. The process involves carefully pulling and stretching the material and the use of hot adhesives. This is when the big mistakes tend to happen.

On the big day, unfortunately a mistake had happened.

The samples went through all the processes and finally arrived in the shoe room for inspection. Someone spotted that some hot adhesive had accidentally dripped onto the uppers. These were made of a synthetic material, like a velvety leopard print. The glue had stuck to it. It was impossible to pull it off because it would tear all the fibres out of it. Disaster! The only remedy was a total re-make from start to finish.

I knew nothing about this; I was in the office filming a short section about the history of the company. Half way through there was a knock at the door. I was a bit annoyed because I had given strict instructions not to be disturbed.

The main Producer motioned for me to keep talking while they continued filming. I was a bit perplexed at this time. I didn't know why they wanted to carry on.

I said, "Come in." Tony one of my managers walked in with an armful of the samples.
"Steve, I wonder if you'd look at this; we've got a problem. The samples are ruined."
Then it clicked. I was furious. "Stop the filming. That's it." I went into full diva mode!

Without telling me, they'd actually asked Tony to come and interrupt my 'to camera' interview, to add a bit more drama, so they could see my reaction. I couldn't believe that they'd tried such a cheap trick. I was absolutely livid.

The fact that they'd done this was nothing short of underhand, deliberately planning a cheap reaction. For me that was the first breach of the agreement and it was then that I felt used and now knew exactly what they were capable of. If they were doing this to me at this early stage, what could they do in the future, not only to me, but also to the workforce, the customers, everyone?

"Right that's it. You're never doing that to me again, you've burned your bridges, I'm not doing it." I saw red.

Then Michele Kurland, who was the Assistant Producer said, "I'm really sorry, the Producer really wanted to do this. I know she shouldn't have done it. Can you leave it with me?"

"OK, but I'm not working with her anymore." I was fuming, and I meant it. "She's completely ruined my trust in her and in this programme."

After the dust had settled, the Producer strategically left early and went back to London. With Michele's sincere apology accepted and her reassurance that it wouldn't happen again, I agreed to give them a second chance and to continue with the programme.

From that moment on Michele took over as the Programme Producer. As it turned out it was the making of the project because she and I had this natural bond. She was a lovely lady, so understanding. She had empathy with what we were doing and what we were trying to do. I felt I could trust her because she was making something serious and not just a sensational reality show.

Michele said they really needed to film Tony showing me the ruined samples, as it was part of what happens in real life manufacturing.

She said, "We'd like to film your reaction and your disappointment because, presumably, you now have to remake the samples from scratch."

"All right, if you must." I was still a bit sore.
Michele realised this and tried to pacify me. "How would you like to give the performance of your life?"
Now what, I thought.
"We won't be able to come back to film the new samples being made. So…"
"So…? What do you want to do?"
"Would you mind changing your shirt and tie and then we'll pretend it's a few days later."

There was no way to get out of it! After my quick change, we acted our socks off! Tony holding the damaged samples, me with my hands and fingers strategically covering the damage. No one would ever know that the damaged ones weren't the new, remade, finished samples!

The finished clips showed me saying to Tony, "If we'd only paid greater attention the first time round, we'd have saved ourselves a lot of trouble and the samples would have looked as good as these." That's another reason not to believe all you see on TV; not everything you see is what it seems.

The samples were duly despatched and the next day we had David on the phone; he was the guy we'd seen in London for the first filmed sales pitch of the Kinky Boots and shoes.

He was over the moon. He thought they were absolutely fantastic and he decided to use them for his new catalogue.

Not only that, but they matched a leopard bikini he was selling. He was going to use our boots and shoes on the front page of his new catalogue.

It was just too good to be true; our first sales samples were a success. We'd already hit the front page AND he was ready to place his first order!

Kinky Boots were up and running, excuse the pun!

"The art of making sexy footwear is like letting your imagination loose in a sweet shop when you're on a diet!!"
Steve Pateman

VII

Boss in Boots!

Jenny, my designer, and I had a brainstorming session so that we could have a clear picture of what lay ahead. One thing was certain; we had to have a good catalogue. Although the Internet was in existence it wasn't as widely in use as it is now. Back then we relied on the printed word, and that meant mail-shots and newspapers for our advertising, backed up with a really good catalogue.

"We need some photos and glamour shots." Jenny was right, that had to be our starting point. We had the sample boots, but we were the only people who knew what they looked like. "Some glam shots showing the full range. That's a must." She added.
"OK," I agreed. I obviously needed all the help I could get now. "How do we go about doing a photo shoot?"
"Well, for a start you find a good photographer, you hire a studio, engage some models, select the footwear and sort out a few 'props' and you're away."

It sounded easy, but once again, our budget was limited. It had to be a professional-looking, but cut-price, catalogue. Sara had done a course in photography at Wellingborough Technical College and had some contacts. In fact her lecturer was a retired wedding photographer; he must have the talent and he might offer his services for a small fee. I made the call.

"I hope you don't mind, but my wife Sara gave me your number. You may remember her; you taught her some photography basics on one of your evening courses. I'm looking for someone who can photograph models wearing some of our footwear for a new catalogue. Is this something you'd be interested in doing?"

"Oh yes, I've done a lot of weddings and so on. I'm used to temperamental brides and excited little bridesmaids, so models should be a snip."

"Well, there's something I must tell you. This isn't exactly like doing wedding photos. It involves scantily clad models in PVC clothing, high-heeled shoes and boots, the odd set of hand-cuffs and whips. Are you still interested?"

I heard some very deep breathing and a long sigh on the other end of the phone followed by an instant, enthusiastic, "Yes, I think I could manage that!"

"What about your fee?" I was still conscious of our budget.

"Oh I don't think we need worry too much about that. I'm retired, so, as long as I cover my costs and a bit left over for a few beers, I'm your man. It sounds like fun and a new challenge."

"Brilliant, I'll get back to you with a date and a venue."

So that was sorted, but already I had visions of something out of a 'Carry On' film; I could see a retired wedding photographer who was used to vicars and blushing brides! After all, it's a long way from church bells and confetti to leather gear, whips and Kinky Boots.

Hiring a studio might be expensive, so phoning around was the next on the list of jobs to be done.

"What's wrong with doing the shoot here, in the factory? It's the perfect setting." Jenny suggested, "Something rather sexy about a skimpily clad woman draped over a big machine."

"Hang on," I said. "One step at a time. We're not making a pin-up calendar!"

Actually, Jenny was right. It seemed obvious. With a bit of careful planning we could use the Board Room as the dressing area and right next to it was a large room full of stock. We could easily clear that and create a studio. So that was another item off the tick-list. But we still needed the model.

I thought of Bev; she'd been so helpful modelling the original samples. It was worth asking her if she'd do the shoot but bless her, as I half expected, she said a polite "No".

"It was all very well doing it in the factory," Bev said, "but the thought of featuring in brochures all over the world in sexy gear was taking it a bit far."

"Wise girl," I thought.

In my research looking through those brochures and catalogues, all the competition seemed to sell more clothing and accessories than boots and shoes. It seemed to me that if we were making the sexy footwear, we could create our own collection of clothes and accessories and offer a complete look.

If customers could see the right shoes with the right outfit, they were more likely to buy it all from me. It made good business sense and anyway, I'd already started to source a lot of PVC clothing, leather underwear, whips and so on.

I remembered a catalogue sent to me by a manufacturer in Nottingham who was hoping to supply us with leather clothing. He'd used a tall, stunning, sultry, dark-haired model; I wondered if she could be the face of our new brand. It was worth a phone call to him.

"I must admit Steve, W.J. Brookes and the sex industry don't always come in the same sentence." He laughed. I suppose I would have to get used to the corny comments. "But I know the girl you mean. Believe it or not she's training to be a nurse, I wonder if she'd still be interested. Hang on, I'm looking for her number as I speak."

Her name was Jane and, when I phoned, by a stroke of luck she was at home.

"I'd love to do it. I'll do it for 'mate's rates'; my accommodation and travel, OK? By the way, I love heels, the higher the better. As long as I can bring a couple of pairs home as well," she laughed, "I'm in."

"It's a deal, can't wait to see you. I'll get back to you with the details."

It was all coming together. She told me her clothing and foot sizes but said she ought to try the boots and shoes on, could we send the samples? So we did. Then disaster! Jane rang up.

"They're fabulous, but huge! I could get both of my legs in one boot; I look like I'm wearing my dad's fishing waders. Honestly, I couldn't wear them for the photo shoot, I'd look ridiculous."

The problem was we'd made the samples for what we considered to be an average sized woman's legs; we wanted to fit as many as possible. The trouble with a model's legs is they tend to be a lot thinner than the average woman's.

There was no alternative. To make them look good on Jane, we would have to re-make all the samples to her leg measurements. So that was going to set us back yet another couple of weeks.

In the meantime, we got on with planning the shoot. The Board Room was converted to a changing room, and our store-room next to it became the studio. It seemed a good arrangement.

Then I thought of all my illustrious, bearded Victorian ancestors staring down from the photo gallery round the Boardroom. The sight of this glamorous model might cause them to come crashing to the floor! Then I thought, 'Hey, let's give them a thrill!'

I'd become so carried away with the thought of the gorgeous Jane, I'd almost forgotten about the men's range. Who was going to model the boots for the cross-dressers and the drag queens? They were the very reason for doing all this in the first place. It was so important to show the men's sizes and how they looked in the catalogue.

Was it too late now? Could I find anyone locally? No way, not if I wanted keep my friends! Then Jenny, my designer, piped up.
"Am I right in thinking all the production samples have been made for a size eleven?"
"Yes." I answered cautiously.
"And, is there the remotest chance that you are a size eleven?"
"You know damn well I am."
"So?" She looked me up and down with a huge grin on her face.
"So?" I responded innocently. I knew bloody well what was coming next.
'So, Mr Size Eleven, you can be the model for the photo shoot."

Jenny stood there sniggering to herself. "Dah-ling, you'll slay 'em!"
"Really? I don't think so!!"
"Of course you will. You'll have to. Anyway it's too late to make them all again for someone else. We have the boots, you are size eleven, you have the legs and you're the boss. It's only waist down, remember."

So Bert was right all along; his words rang in my ears. "It's your bloody idea, do it yerself."

I took a deep breath, deep enough to swim the channel; a feat that at this moment sounded considerably more attractive. "Make or break time," I'd been telling everybody. Now was the time for me to step up to the mark.

"There you go Boss, there's your home-work for tonight," Jenny pointed to the men's Kinky Boots, "stand in front of the mirror; get your posing right, then tomorrow you can show me what you've got. Remember. Now you're a model!" She walked out killing herself laughing.

"You're enjoying this aren't you?" I shouted after her.
"You bet! Just a bit, it's called 'pay-back'. Enjoy!!" Her laughs echoing down the hallway.
I arrived home and Sara helped me put the boots on. She held my hands and it was like it was when she held our son Dan by the fingers as he took his first steps. Only this time it was me in my four-and-a-half inch heels. She started to give me advice.

"Come on. Strengthen your core. Clench your bum cheeks. Stand up straight, shoulders back. Oh, and by the way, try and look sexy!"

In a moment of over confidence, I broke free from her vice-like grip and tottered too far and fell flat on my face. In fact that happened a couple of times and, I'm amused to say, it became one of the classic scenes later in the film and the musical. In the 'fashion show' scene in Milan I, renamed Charlie Price, made a right fool of myself on the catwalk and, in front of hundreds of top fashion buyers, fell flat on my face. True to form!

Eventually I could manage a few paces without flattening my nose on the floor. It was a case of learning how to walk again. The normal 'heel down first' just doesn't work in high heels unless you want a twisted ankle! Positioning was crucial and placing the ball of the foot and heel down at the same time is a must. A strong tightening of the calves and thighs and tucking the bum in was essential.

It was when I put the court shoes on that Sara collapsed with laughter yet again. She noticed something that really had to be sorted. My hairy rugby-playing legs!

"You can't model court shoes with legs like that. No self-respecting cross-dresser would be seen dead with hairy legs. You've got to shave them."
"You can forget that!" I barked dismissively, "perhaps I'll speak to Jenny and see what we can come up with."

Sara was right, there was no way I could model the shoes with legs like mine! The hair had to come off; Jenny agreed. The girls had spoken!

It just so happened that I was talking to Michele on the phone about the up and coming filming when I happened to let slip in a jokey way that I was going to have to shave my legs to model the boots and shoes.

"I love it," she was in hysterics, "we must to film it. I can see the headline; 'Boss shaves his legs and models Kinky Boots to save business!' Priceless!"

"No way! I'll do most things, but I must keep some of my dignity. After all, I am the Boss of a company of eighty people. There are some things a man has to do in private"

But then she tried the bribery.

"Hang on Steve," she thought for a minute, "we'll put you up in a London hotel, treat you to a show, give you a five star meal, all you have to do is shave your legs to camera."

Tempted as I was, I knew it was a step too far. If it was going to be done, it had to be my bath tub, a pack of Bic razors, a locked bathroom door and me.

The time had come. Another step into the realms of uneasiness. I'd seen how Sara did it. Simple; it's a piece of cake really, nothing complicated; I'm used to shaving my face every day; what's the big deal?

I went upstairs, filled the bath, poured half a jar of Sara's best bubble bath into the steaming water. The fragrant wave of exotic aromas filled the room and an inch-deep layer of white foam evoked a tropical beach with crashing waves. My mind wandered to the telly ads of a seductive woman with her toe resting on the tap while shaving her smooth, golden, sun-kissed legs! But now it was my turn.

As I slowly lowered myself into the bubbles, thoughts of the last time I had a bath flashed across my mind. It was after the rugby game on Saturday. From beer and belching in a communal bath tub to soft scented suds in my own bathroom. How could two worlds be so different? I was about to cross from one world to another!!

It was a journey I couldn't put off any longer. I took the first razor from the pack; my leg all lathered, rested on the tap. It was now or never. My hand was poised like a surgeon about to make his first incision. I stroked my leg with the blade in a long sweeping motion, but after scraping only an inch the hair clogged the razor and the first drops of blood mingled with the white suds.

I grabbed another razor and repeated the operation, so much for it being a quick job. Three-quarters of an hour later, I rose from the depths of the cold bath water like a phoenix from the ashes. The bath now told a different story. A brown, shag-pile carpet had replaced the white foam as though someone had just shaved a bear. The rim of the bath was littered with spattered blood and blunt razors. Was this the price women had to pay to have beautiful legs?

I gazed down at what was left of my legs. They looked and felt cold; amazing, but cold, very cold and WHITE! White like a fillet of cod before it hits the batter. White like a Polar Bear's armpit. White like the last albino chicken that's been plucked by Colonel Sanders ready for one of his KFC bucket deals! My legs were white!

Then came the next bright idea. In the bathroom cupboard was another forbidden fruit. The fake tan. Remembering how Sara used it at the approach of spring to make her legs look lightly tanned, I took it and, without a second thought, I poured some into my hands and slapped it onto my legs and thighs again and again until both my legs had been completely covered.

I looked down. It hadn't worked. My legs remained as white as ever. They must be in need of a second coat. I put on some more of the evil-smelling lotion, but this time, more generously to make sure it worked.

There was still no change. Had I missed something in the instructions that, like a typical man, I hadn't read until now?

And there it was. "Your tan will start to develop over the next 45 minutes onwards." Hell!

As I'd bent over to apply the stuff to my ankles, it had gone everywhere including the bits that never see the sun, if you get my meaning! And a strange tingling sensation started to develop from my toes, up my ankles, calves and thighs, with an increasingly burning sensation, especially around the meat and two veg.

A glance in the mirror told me my legs were gradually getting darker and darker; by now they were already deep mahogany, they looked as if they'd be perfect on a Victorian grand piano!

There was no way I could let them get any darker. Panic! I quickly emptied the bath, scraped up as much of the hair from round the tub as I could, filled the bath again, grabbed the loofah and tried to scrub the remaining tanning lotion off. I rubbed them raw trying to transform my legs from what had now turned the darkest ebony, to the smooth golden, sun-kissed colour of those telly ads.

Thankfully, the stinging subsided, and some form of normality started to return. Just then from downstairs, I heard Sara calling.

"Don't forget, if you're shaving your legs, you might need to put a little tanning lotion on afterwards. But be careful, it's strong stuff, so, for heaven's sake, make sure you read the instructions."

As if I wouldn't...!!!

"When a man shaves his legs a whole new world of possibilities opens up before him. Like putting on my first pair of high-heeled shoes and having to learn how to walk again."
Steve Pateman

VIII

The Photo Shoot

The next day Jenny demanded her own little fashion show to see what my shaved and tanned legs looked like. Much to her amusement she said, "They look quite good; they could actually pass."

Then we had to sort out the arrangements for the photo shoot. We cleared all the tables and chairs out of the Board Room and I made a big dressing area. I'd never actually met Jane so I wanted to make sure she'd got everything she needed.

I borrowed the mirrors from Sara's dressing table; we provided bottles of water, a hairdryer, everything she might require. The Board Room was always kept clean, but it wasn't clean enough, so we gave every corner of the skirting board and ceiling an extra special 'once-over', even with the long attachment on the vacuum cleaner.

Jenny and I had spent almost two weeks making meticulous lists and running orders ready for the shoot, plus detailed notes of what Jane was to wear.

We needed hundreds of photographs for the catalogue, with lots of props and changes of clothes and footwear. We indexed all the clothes and boots with numbers so we knew what items of clothing went with which footwear and which accessory.

It was a mammoth task, but it really paid off, and when later professional models came to do a shoot with us, they were amazed at how organised our system was.

It was a case of running it like a well-oiled machine; a stage show that had to go without any hiccups, because the last thing we wanted was for the BBC to think we were a bunch of amateurs.

This all happened, remember, in the 1990s. If we'd done it now, we'd have had computers and spread sheets but then, for us, it was just pens, pads, index lists and a lot of sticky labels!

The day of the shoot arrived. It was a Saturday when the factory was quiet with no one else around. I collected Jane from the station.

"Welcome to W.J. Brookes, The Kinky Boot Factory, I said, as I helped her in with her cases, "and welcome to Earls Barton."

"Thanks, nice to be here." Smiled Jane.
"Let's go in and I'll show you round."

We had a quick look at the factory and the machinery as we passed and then I showed her where she could dress. I was very proud of what we'd done for her; the dressing-table looked terrific with standard lamps and mirrors, so she could do her make-up.

"Hey Steve, you've thought of everything, it's smashing." Great, I thought, that's a good start.
"If there's anything else you need, just ask, OK?"
"Thanks."

We showed her the boots and shoes, the clothing and props, everything set out neatly. Then we went into the 'studio'. We'd managed to get hold of a huge roll of white paper, the sort they use in professional studios. We'd hung it from some tripods and draped it on the floor so there were no hard edges showing, it really did look brilliant.

"We've found a good photographer for you, he'll be here in a minute." I had my fingers crossed in my pocket, hoping against hope that he was up to the job. "He's not the usual sort of fashion photographer you're probably used to. He's more used to doing weddings. Portraits, you know?"

"That's OK, I've worked with all sorts. A photographer's a photographer; I'm sure we'll work round it. I'm not one of those models who has to have everything perfect; I just do it for the fun."

I sighed, "I reckon we're going to get on just fine." What a relief!

We had a quick look round to make sure everything was ready. The BBC were going to arrive half-way through the photo shoot, so we wanted to get the bulk of it done before they turned up.

The photographer, Harold, arrived with his camera and all his lighting gear and started to set up. I had totally misjudged how old he was; I'd expected perhaps a man in his mid-sixties. He turned out to be more late sixties, early seventies; he was still very able and agile, but not the typical trendy 'click, click, click' fashion snapper!

I wondered how he'd react to Jane suddenly appearing in little more than a pair of high heels! The last thing I wanted was to see him keel over on the floor with a heart attack and an ambulance arriving, with him coming round and a scantily clad woman in a leather bikini standing over him. He might think he'd died and gone to heaven!

I left him sorting out his gear and went into the Board Room where Jane was making herself at home, laying out her make-up and brushes on the table.

"Can I show you the outfit for the first shots? It's all ready for you. Here's a running order with all the clothes and footwear so you know what to wear and when."
"Wow, I don't usually get treated like this, it's great, thanks."
"If you'd like to get yourself ready, I'll go and check with Harold and then we can start."
I stopped and stood in the passage between the Board Room and the make-shift studio. I was all on edge, nervous with anticipation; I couldn't really believe this was happening, but it was, and I was in the middle of it. It was something unbelievably exciting, terrifying, unreal and electrifying. For a moment it was as though I was on the outside looking in.

"Are you OK?" Jenny, clip-board in hand had appeared from nowhere and was looking slightly quizzically at me.
"It's actually happening Jenny."
"I know. Crazy isn't it? How's Jane doing?"
"She's nearly ready, I'll just check with the photographer and then we can crack on."

Harold was ready and waiting, so back I went to the Board Room. I knocked gently on the door.

"OK if I come in?" I wanted to do things right, I didn't want to barge in and embarrass her.
"Yea, come in. Everything's fine, no probs!!"

The door swung open and as I walked into the Board Room I was met with this gorgeous, glamorous girl standing absolutely stark naked in front of me.

I felt myself looking anywhere except at Jane. I knew the Board Room was spotlessly clean, but I was looking round at the floor hoping to see a paper clip, a speck of dust, or cobwebs in the ceiling; anything but Jane.

All I could see were the oak framed photographs of my Dad, Grandad and severe looking Great Grandfather, staring down at me. If it happened now, it would make me think of all those portraits in Harry Potter's 'Hogwarts' stories. I half expected them to clamp their hands over their eyes and run out of their frames in utter disbelief. Their ghostly voices crying, "Steve, Steve, what are you doing? A naked woman in our Board Room?"

Back to reality. The red heat of embarrassment was taking me over yet again. Jane was giggling.

"This is your first one isn't it? You're a 'photo shoot virgin'. I'm going to have fun with you!" She obviously felt relaxed enough to be taking the micky out of me, laughing as the red in my face turned to bright scarlet. I was like a thermometer in boiling water, fit to burst.

"Y-e-s." My voice cracked, it was almost a cough. She just smiled and got on with dressing.

That was it. The ice had been broken. After all, we were paying her and a photographer for the day. For her it was just another shoot, she was used to all this. I had to be just as professional and get on with the job.

On the floor beside me I saw the bra she had to wear for the first picture, I bent over and picked it up between my thumb and forefinger and handed it to her as if I was handing her a smelly rugby sock that had just been discovered at the bottom of my kit bag; my head was buried deep into my chest trying not to look.

"I think you need this."
"Thanks." She turned round and held the bra to her chest, "Well, while you're here do me up, can you?"
I cleared my throat. "Sure." She pushed the cups to her boobs. "Pull really tight, Steve, I've got to get the cleavage just right."
She turned round to face me. "Now, what d'you reckon?"
"Lovely, yes, they look…lovely."
"I mean the bikini, Steve!" Could my face get any redder? "We'll make a pro out of you yet!" she smiled.

She had that evil glint in her eye. Totally harmless, but powerful! She was really playing with my emotions, but I was beginning to realise she had a wicked sense of humour and I loved it!

Now she was fully dressed, I could relax a bit. It was strange; within minutes I was completely at ease with her. She obviously had no embarrassment so why should I?

So having been the pathetic, coy, worried bloke who didn't want to turn red, within half an hour I was helping her get into tight tops, pushing bits of her anatomy in and up, hoisting straps, zipping up her thigh-length boots. Jane was just lovely. She knew she was in charge; she led and she was clearly impressed with how smoothly it all went.

We had to laugh, though, when she made her first entrance into the studio. Harold, the photographer took one look and almost fell backwards into his tripod. He was obviously a bit overwhelmed by what he saw.

"Well, yes, I haven't done one of these before, but I suppose it's the same as a bride!" he muttered with a Sid James type of leering smile straight out of a Carry On film.

I could see the same glow of red start to spread over his face. Harold's finger was now running round the inside of his shirt collar doing that imaginary release of heat that seemed trapped around his neck; eventually he managed to regain his cOmposure and normal service resumed. Thank goodness I wasn't the only one who seemed to get embarrassed.

He was a true professional, albeit, not quite in his comfort zone. The photo shoot continued. There was just one thing though, Jane was used to the photographer telling her what to do. 'Pout', 'bend', 'put your boobs together', 'hold your hand in the air'. Whereas our photographer was more, 'would you mind doing this, my dear?' or 'that's lovely, sweetie, hold it…splendid.'

For Jane the camera had always clicked away while she moved up, down, in, out, round and round, flicking her hair, and so on; today it was more a case of, 'y-e-s, that's nice, h-o-l-d it, click!'

The extraordinary thing was that when we finally had all the photographs developed and Jane came back to see them, she couldn't believe the standard of the shots. Usually at professional photo sessions there'd be thirty shots out of which one might be good, but here, Harold had taken, for example, three shots and we got two really good ones. It was amazing.

We did well with our morning's work and the bulk of it was done before the BBC arrived. On their arrival we really did look like a professional outfit and the rest of the shoot went off with no hitches.

Jane worked brilliantly with them, but I was the one they really wanted to film. The tables were turned when it was my turn to dress and pose. Now Jenny and Jane were the ones zipping me up and pulling my legs into position. Now I was the person who was being manhandled!

Yet again I was asking myself, "Am I doing the right thing? Should a boss be doing his own modelling?" I was beginning to make myself embarrassed now. The boss standing in his rugby shorts, legs shaved and tanned, wearing all manner of high-heeled shoes and boots. Hello?

The BBC cameras were recording every move! It was too late. All I wanted was for the floor to open up and swallow me; but I was committed. Perhaps I should have been committed! There was no turning back now.

When I first appeared in the studio on the white paper in thigh length boots with four-and-a-half inch heels, on an uncarpeted floor, I did look as though I was going to fall flat on my face; once again I felt like Bambi on stilts taking his first wobbly steps. When Jane posed it looked easy, but in my case Sara's instructions rang in my ears, "Keep your back upright, tuck your bum in, straighten your legs, look sexy!"

In reality it looked as if I was about to crumple in a heap on the floor. Jane now came into her element, giving me stage directions, posing tips, positioning and placing my legs and feet, trying to make me look like a model.

Thank goodness the factory was empty. If the good people of Earls Barton could have seen me now! Thank goodness it was only us; the BBC cameras and, later…four-and-a-half million viewers!

Sara and my two-and-a-half-year-old son, Dan, had been standing in the 'wings' all through the filming, enjoying the spectacle, laughing at my gangly poses and my efforts to look sexy!!

On the Monday after the shoot, Dan had a wonderful time telling his preschool mates about his new 'auntie' called Jane who likes to wear skimpy clothing and his dad wearing thigh length boots with someone taking pictures of them!

He was so proud boasting about his exciting weekend's activity, we were dreading a call from his Head Teacher asking us what on earth had been going on! Luckily this was one phone call we managed to avoid.

Harold took hundreds of pictures, far more than we needed; this was well before the age of digital photography. In those days a camera had a roll of film that had to be sent away to be developed. This could often take up to a week or more before the photographs would arrive back in an envelope along with the processed negatives. Now, of course, we can see the picture instantly on our phones or digital cameras. Even with those delays the photo shoot was the easy bit. The real work was just about to begin.

We had to design the catalogue, edit it, arrange it, give every product a code number and price; the layout had to be just right. I was anxious that it had to be perfect and had to be the right size.

Most suppliers in this business had an A4 catalogue but my idea was to have an A5, half the size of A4. It would be cheaper to post and easier for the customer to slip it into a pocket, handbag or even under the pillow!

Having the catalogue finished in time to catch our potential customers was going to be a tall order. We knew that Düsseldorf in September was a firm booking, and I had also booked a stand at the end of November at the UK's most important exhibition of fetish and sexy clothing, footwear and accessories. It had to be ready to launch then.

So we had deadlines; it was going to be extremely tight. It was then or not at all. These two events would be our first experience of meeting the public and selling to our new potential customers. Düsseldorf was one thing; we'd done it before, without the BBC cameras of course and we knew the ropes. But the show in November was something totally new and very different.

It would be Kinky Boots on show to customers who were 100% on our side and, with a fabulous catalogue to take home, ready to buy. We hoped! The exhibition was called 'Erotica'.

"I have been photographed in so many high heels but never in my Brogues."
Steve Pateman

IX

Return to Düsseldorf: The Relaunch Take 2!

The September show in Düsseldorf was important for all British exhibitors, not just us. We were all suffering from cheap imports. It was something we'd seen on the horizon for some time, but now it was becoming pretty critical.

I've already mentioned that we were on the brink of disaster. The boot and shoe industry was going through a really hard time. A small company like ours faced an uncertain and bleak future knowing that if orders for our regular lines didn't pickup and fast, we'd have to cut down on staff and then, if the worst came to the worst, we'd have to close the factory.

I was determined this wasn't going to happen on my watch. That is why this next show in Germany had to be successful for us, or that black cloud might descend on us sooner than we had feared.

Being young and keen I'd become involved quite heavily with The Footwear Federation. At every meeting I attended, there was one big on-going problem at the top of the agenda. The British boot and shoe industry was suffering because of cheap imports that were beginning to flood the UK market. How would we make people aware of this?

It was, in many ways, more of a local problem than a national one. You see, Northamptonshire was the boot and shoe capital of the UK and had built its universal reputation for making expensive top of the range shoes, as well as being world leaders in designer and street fashion footwear.

It was the age of Carnaby Street, Kings Road, Vivienne Westwood and the pop revolution. London was the fashion centre of the world and Northamptonshire's shoe factories were crucial in shaping the future of street fashion.

If you walk down Burlington Arcade or Jermyn Street in London's Mayfair, you'll still see the exclusive shoe shops that attract the rich and famous. Great names like Church's, Cheaney, Crockett and Jones, Edward Green, John Lobb, Loake's, Jeffery-West and our close neighbours, Barker's of Earls Barton. All those shops sell shoes with 'Made in Northampton' printed inside.

Most of those companies sold abroad and even though we were a much smaller concern, we too relied heavily on export and we'd feel the sting just as much as they would, if not more, should the orders stop.

As the time for the shoe fair in Germany approached we drew up a plan for our stand and, as well as our normal stock, we made room for a larger display of the Kinky Boots. I contacted Jane our catalogue model, since all the samples had been made to her size and measurements, we really needed her.

"How would you like to have a weekend away in Düsseldorf?"

"Love to." She was keen from the start. Stan, one of my managers, came with us. One of our main customers in Düsseldorf had agreed to help and let us stay at his place, which was good because we were still trying to save every penny we could.

We carefully selected our samples and since everything we took had to go through customs, it all had to be packed properly in cartons and despatched a few days before we left.

Our stand at Düsseldorf was 25 square metres in size and was in one of thirteen vast halls. We tend to think of England as the shoe capital of the world, but when you see these halls packed with shoe manufacturers from every country of the globe, you feel like a needle in a haystack.

When we turned up for the first day of the show, things didn't look too good. We had no electrics on the stand, the cleaners hadn't tidied it and we were there with a grotty mess all over our brand new carpets. Without power my hi-tech moving lights, sound system and computer were useless, and our big, lighted branding projection signs were dead in the water. How were we going to cope now?

For the BBC team, who were coming there to film, this was to be another terrific opportunity; so everything had to work. Customers would soon be pouring in. The tension was mounting. Cameras would soon be rolling, and there I was, complaining to the hall site team, in my best pigeon German.

Eventually with much pleading and begging (and a small bribe) an electrician and cleaner turned up. It was a close call on that first day, but just in time we had power on the stand ready for receiving our potential customers.

The show opened and within minutes it was clear that the interest was colossal. The first time we were there back in the spring we didn't have Jane, only the boots. This time she was with us, ready and willing to walk around looking sultry and sexy. She wore her really tight PVC mini skirt and an even tighter, skimpier top. She had black thigh length PVC boots on, and with her dark hair flowing she looked terrific.

As all the crowds poured into the halls the word got round that there was a television crew filming. Suddenly we were invaded with our own crowd scene! Our stand was absolutely solid with buyers, almost all of whom were blokes and you could see them drooling, tongues hanging out, not interested in anything but Jane and her sexy outfits, they were just standing around waiting for her next costume change. Did we care? No way! We were firing on all cylinders!

The crowds were attracting more crowds; we were the talk of the hall; the word was spreading, and the cameras were rolling. Soon, as well as the 'voyeurs', even the right customers were arriving at the stand. It couldn't have been better.

We became quite friendly with a Turkish seller whose stand was opposite ours; he used to bring us Turkish coffee; you know, the thick, dark stuff full of sugar, which kept us hyper with every sip. He regularly popped over to see how we were doing on the pretence of giving us more coffee, at least that's what he said. In fact, like the rest of them, he just wanted to get a closer look at Jane.

"Steve," he said once in his broken English, "you are such a PR man, fancy having a fake TV crew to film and get people to stop and look at your stand, what a brilliant idea."
"No it's real," I said, "honestly'.
"Yea, yea, yea" he answered in his best Turkish-English accent and in total disbelief. We couldn't get him to realise that they were a real TV crew filming for the BBC.

So, all in all, the show was a huge success. We had more contacts, far more interest and far more potential orders than we could ever have dreamed of. Some eight hundred pairs of Kinky Boots and shoes were ordered and dozens of samples for us to make for our new customers. We knew that, with the extra pressure of the new samples in the kinky department, we were going to be flat out over the next few weeks.

Michele and the camera crew came up to Northamptonshire again with plans to do more filming inside and outside the factory. This time they wanted me to assemble my managers and foremen in the Board Room to bring them up to date with how successful the Düsseldorf show had been and the extra work that faced us.

The BBC had come up with a great idea; they wanted to film the meeting through the Board Room windows with my silhouetted back to the camera.

"How are you going to do that?" I was curious. "The Board Room is on the first floor, are you putting the camera man on stilts?"

"In a way," Michele said, "We'll bring a platform crane up from London and then we'll park it by the crossroads at King Street and North Street. On the crane will be the camera operator and we'll raise it up and film from the outside looking in through the window. It'll look good with the camera over your shoulders looking at your workers as you tell them of your success at Düsseldorf."

What a waste of money. "Surely we've got cranes in Northampton, you don't have to bring one up from London."
"No, it has to come from London. Health and safety and all that."

So they brought a massive crane up from London. Now what I must explain is that where our factory was in King Street, it's a very tight squeeze; North Street, Queen Street and King Street are all narrow Victorian side streets with our factory on one corner. You'd struggle to get two cars through side-by-side, let alone a crane!

It seems they'd done a 'recce' and couldn't park the crane outside the factory because the arms wouldn't stretch across to look through the window at the right angle. So they parked it at the top end of North Street and they put the arms of the crane up. They had to stretch across the corner of the garden of the house opposite the factory to get the right view through the window. It looked quite safe and out of the way of traffic, so we thought nothing more about it.

On the crane's platform were the crew; a camera-man, producer, a runner with a radio, sound operator and Michele.

Picture this. There I am sitting at the head of the table with my managers and foremen down each side, but what you couldn't see is what was underneath the table. This was where the sound technician, the guy with the boom mic and the runner with the radio had to be hidden out of camera shot. They had to be there in order to synchronise what was going on outside with what was happening inside the Board Room.

This then was the plan. "We'll give you a knock on the table when we want you to start," said the man with the radio from under the table, "and you do your speech to the guys, OK?"

There was no speech. I was just going to talk off the top of my head, like I did most the time! So there came a knock on the table, and I started.

"Guys, it's fantastic news. Stan and I had a brilliant time in Düsseldorf and we've sold over 800 pairs of our new range plus our usual orders; we've got loads of business cards from all over the world and if we can fill these first orders and the numerous samples we've been asked for, we're going to be so busy…"

Then a knock on the table. I peeked underneath to the runner with the radio.

"What's up?"
"Oh, slight technical problem. Camera and sound weren't synchronised, we're going to have to do it again."

Another knock on the table. Another start of my spiel.

"Look guys, we're just back from Dusseldorf and it's great news…"

Another knock on the table.

"For goodness sake what is it this time?" This is the BBC, can't they get it right?
"Another technical hitch, can you go again?"

By now I was wearying and my voice must have reflected the fact.

"Right guys, back from Düsseldorf, great success, 800 hundred pairs, business cards…" My speech was getting shorter and shorter each time and considerably less enthusiastic. I was desperate to get my guys back to the factory floor working again.

My managers and foremen thought this was hilarious and were trying hard to make me laugh, but I was getting really hacked off by now; I felt really angry.

AND, YES, another knock on the table.
"Oh come on, I don't believe it. Now what?"
"Sorry Steve, we've got problems outside."

So we all turned and looked out of the window and there was a most incredible sight. It was like a scene out of a 'Monty Python' sketch. There was a man, who clearly wasn't going to put up with any nonsense, standing in his garden.

He was a retired old chap, who probably fought in both World Wars and everything in between. His house was directly opposite the factory. He was standing there with two walking sticks; he was leaning on one and waving the other madly in the air at the crew in the crane above. So we opened the window.

What on earth was going on? There he was shouting at the top of his voice. "I don't give a toss who or what you are, you can be the Queen of England for all I care, just get that crane thing out of my airspace."

And there's poor Michele pleading in her best BBC voice, "But we're from the BBC. We're filming over the road."

"I don't give damn where you're from, you can go and do it elsewhere." He ranted in his old Barton drawl, "You are not filming in my airspace. Go on the lot o' yer, Bugger off!"

So this amazing old man made the whole operation come to a standstill. The might of the BBC had met the might of a local Bartoner. In all the time I'd been working with the BBC I'd never seen them back down, but they were forced to dismantle the crane. They had to re-site it in a position that didn't encroach on his airspace or cast a shadow over his prize leeks! It was hysterical. I was killing myself laughing as the BBC crew, with their proverbial tail between their proverbial legs, retreated to a safe distance.

Final Score: Bartoners: One ~ BBC : Nil!

We eventually finished filming, but I felt something was missing. The BBC had planned to finish the programme with the success at Düsseldorf as the grand finale, but I knew it wanted more. It was incomplete.

"Look Michele," we were enjoying a welcome cup of tea after the final shoot, "We've done all the processes, we've done some marketing, we've done the Düsseldorf show, but I still think we need something more sensational."

She looked interested and slightly hurt, perhaps thinking I was being critical. "What more do we need?"
"Well look, I've spent all this money to invest in our launch. Although we've done well at Düsseldorf, our catalogue is aimed at a particular section of the public. Surely we need to have a real ending for the programme that must be about the page three girls, drag queens, cross-dressers and all the other people we're supplying," I paused to take a breath! "Honestly, I think the programme is incomplete. The viewer doesn't care a toss about the commercial side, the businessmen and the companies, all they want to see are the hidden secrets, the behind the scenes shows, the juicy bits."

"So what do you suggest?"

I could sense a hint of defeat in her voice. I knew I had to be positive.

"Look Michele, very soon the Erotica exhibition is on at Olympia in London. Since it's one of the largest and most prestigious venues in Britain it's going to get thousands of visitors each day. We've got a massive stand, something like eighty square metres. It'll be full of Kinky Boots, our full range that we've been making for these people. I reckon you're missing a trick if you don't come and film that. What's more, you need to see the people, the interaction between the product and the customer. You need to see the way the Kinky Boots come to life. After all, they're the stars!"

Her eyes lit up, I could see she was warming to the idea, but it seemed her boss had told her there was no more budget to do any more filming. They could do what had been planned and budgeted for, but no more.

But I knew Michele had taken on board what I'd said. As it was now, there was no good ending to the story. The journey of Kinky Boots had been told so far, but there was no really explosive climax!!

It wasn't long before we had the answer.

"Steve, I've got some good news."

It was Michele, three days later and in a bubbly mood, "They've agreed, it needs to have an ending that the audience will never forget. We reckon this is it. You in the world of Erotica, modelling the boots face to face with your customers. It'll be great telly. After all, sex sells!"

I was thrilled. Erotica, here we come!

Somehow Michele had managed to arrange the extra budget to film at Erotica. The BBC crew, back in, started editing the footage they'd recorded so far. That gave us time to get back to some real shoe-making to fulfil the orders we'd taken in Düsseldorf and to make and despatch the samples to our potential new customers as well as preparing for our biggest launch; that of our Kinky Boots to the people at the world's sexiest show, Erotica.

Key to our preparation was getting the catalogue put together and printed ready to hand out at the show. Everything was going well, but we still didn't have a brand name.

Throughout the process of my research, I'd been using the term, 'Fetish Footwear' but I soon began to realise that it was too isolating, too 'shocking', literally.

I needed a name that would be softer somehow, that made people want to be part of it, something that wasn't offensive in any way, a name your Granny, your Mum, your Dad, anybody could use without thinking they'd wandered into the back streets of Soho.

I'd had all sorts of names running round in my head and I couldn't see the wood for the trees. Jenny and I had spent hours trying to come up with a brand name, when suddenly she had an idea.

"Steve, it's time you opened your wallet again," she laughed, "let's ask the staff and give a prize to the one who comes up with the best name. It's a good way of keeping them on your side, and who knows, one of them might turnout to be a future customer!"

Some of the workforce put their suggestions on bits of paper and we went through them, knowing that somewhere there could be the perfect name. Wrong! Their suggestions were all sleazy, shocking and sexy in entirely the wrong way. As we read them we realised it was the worst idea we'd ever had.

"All we need," I said as I turned to Jenny, "is a word that's descriptive, sensuous without being sleazy, I can't think of how to say it. An everyday word that people could use without being embarrassed, it has to be out of this world, slightly romantic without being sloppy, like love is…heavenly, love is…divine."

Lights flashed, bells rang, heavenly choirs sang! "That's it! Divine. What d'you think?"
"That's it. It's perfect." Jenny beamed.

"Even better," I gushed excitedly, "because Divine was that famous American drag queen. Do you remember her song, 'You think you're a man'; it was a huge hit. They'll all identify with her; it's…brilliant!! It's Divine."

We started to play on the word, Divine Intervention, Love is Divine, Divine Inspiration, it was absolutely perfect.

At last the concept, the product and the catalogue had a name. All we had to do was make it all a reality.

We'd created Kinky Boots. Now Kinky Boots had a name.

'DIVINE FOOTWEAR'

"Sexy footwear is not just in the design but in the feel of the material, the height of the heel and the admiring looks that they generate."
Steve Pateman

X

The Real World

It was as though I was living two separate lives. Working with the BBC filming 'Trouble at the Top' was like another world.

Back in the real world, Earls Barton and specifically W.J. Brookes, at the factory things weren't so glamorous; in fact they were in dire straits.

The state of the British shoe trade was becoming worse rather than better, with even more of a down-turn in business. New foreign orders were harder to find and harder to secure. The currency exchange rate wasn't becoming any better and our customers were still waiting for it to alter.

If they bought in their footwear at the wrong currency exchange rate then obviously they were paying more for the goods. This would mean they'd make less profit because they still wouldn't be able to pass on the increase in prices to their customers.

Our boots and shoes were really starting to pile up. Even more! Every bit of free space within the factory had cartons stacked, all ready for despatch and waiting to be called in by our customers. Our cash flow was starting to be a problem.

Then we found that an American customer with a history of placing large orders for our fashion shoes was starting to be erratic with payments. He was obviously having problems and we were beginning to worry.

We'd been working with him for a number of years when now his payments slowed down. When we chased him for them he said, "Oh sorry, there must be a problem with the letter of credit or the transfer, I'll get that to you, don't worry."

But worry we did! Unfortunately the next order was already en route. Then came more excuses. In the end he owed us a lot of money. His account was well over the agreed credit limit. Finally he said, "I can't speak to you any more, I've gone into voluntary liquidation." Under American Law this allowed him to declare himself bankrupt.

In these circumstances no one could contact him. We tried hard with solicitors, accountants and the banks, but in the end we lost a considerable sum of money. We had to face reality and decided we had to look at our workforce and think about redundancies.

We'd tried everything else. Even with the huge number of orders for the Kinky range, we'd already put the factory on short time working, but we needed to save more money and obviously we had no choice. The biggest cost to any business is manpower.

We had to do something and quick. Never in the history of the company had we had to cut down on staff. I went through everything with my managers and my Father; we agreed we still had to make the same amount of goods but we needed to make it with fewer people.

In a community like Earls Barton where everybody knows everybody, redundancies have a knock-on effect. I'd worked alongside most of them since I left school at sixteen-and-a-half. A lot had worked alongside my Father. I knew their families, mothers, brothers, sisters even dads and granddads. It's a very hard decision to make, but it's a business decision we had to take.

Obviously, people knew the situation. They weren't stupid. They knew what was happening. Lots and lots of factories had been hit far worse than we had. So far we had been relatively lucky.

I had to speak to the Footwear Union and once they'd approved what we were planning to do, I would have to call the whole factory together for a meeting.

My two managers stood with me in front of the whole workforce. They knew. Their faces told me that they knew. The room was silent. The only sounds you could hear were the machines cooling, the compressed air escaping from the pipes, the old woodwork creaking and my heart beating so loudly I was sure everyone in the room could hear it.

It was the most difficult moment in my life and the hardest speech I'd ever had to make. Still to this day I can't remember exactly what I said because I've tried to block it from my memory, but basically, I said, "We've suffered a large debt from our biggest American customer; he's gone bust. We're going to have to cut costs. If we don't we could lose everything. Therefore, we have no alternative but to try to reduce our overheads. This unfortunately means some job losses."

There was a bit of shuffling of feet. No one spoke. I looked at them all; it was terrible. Even to this day, whenever the thought of that moment crosses my mind, I can feel myself close to tears.

"You know this is something I've never wanted to do, we've looked at everything, but I'm going to have to make seventeen people redundant."

At our peak, when we were at our busiest, we'd had eighty men and women working for us, but with natural wastage of course people leave. We hadn't replaced them. We'd tried to spread the jobs around to save on wages. Anything to stop the inevitable.

How I held the tears back, I'll never know. I'm not normally the sloppy type that cries at movies or sad situations. I can usually control my emotions, but these people were more to me than just employees; they were like family to me. But it had to be done.

"I'll call you in one by one, because I want to talk to you face to face. I'll do everything I can to help you sort out a new job. I'll give you references and help wherever possible."

Nothing could make this any easier. This is something that was included in the film and the musical. Every time I watch them, the emotions flood back; the sadness and the failure; the doubt in my mind; was it my fault? What could I have done differently?

What if…?

But what was wonderful was how accepting most of them were. Had it been me, it would have been a terrible thing to be told, but these lovely people were just amazing.

"We knew it was coming Steve, we had our suspicions," said one, "We know you can't go on like this, you've done everything you can, we know." said another.

In some ways that was the hardest thing to hear. If they had been angry and shouted that it was my fault that they were losing their jobs, it might have been easier to take. But their calm acceptance was so very hard to hear.

I still feel upset when I remember one lad who worked in the lasting room. I called him in and said, "I'm really sorry mate, I've worked with you for many years now and although I don't want to, I've got to make you redundant."

To my surprise he said, "Ah don't worry Steve, I knew all about it. I may not be the sharpest tool in the shed but I knew something was going on. I expected it, don't worry about me; I can get a job anywhere."
"Oh that's really good of you," I answered, "but I still feel awful."
"No," he said, "Don't worry about me. The person I feel sorry for is you, not me."
"What?" I questioned. I didn't understand.

"Well," he said, "put it this way, I can walk into any factory anywhere and I can get a job. They're always looking for people like me…labourers…warehouse work…packing, I can do anything. But what if you lose your job? Can you just walk into another one? There's more opportunities for me, but who's going to want a boss and put him on the factory floor? You're over-qualified for most jobs."

I thanked him for being so loyal and understanding and he went out. I sat down at my desk with my head in my hands and I don't think I've ever cried so much in my life. It really did hit home; it awakened all those feelings that had probably been building up for ages. The fact that they'd all been so damn nice. Oh, there were one or two who said, "Yea, whatever!" but the majority really acknowledged that I'd done everything I could. Some even said I should be proud, which just made it worse.

How can you be proud when you've hit the lives of so many in such a small community? OK, we'd tried hard not to dismiss more than one member in a family, but it didn't always work. We had to think about the distribution of skills in the factory and, in some cases, sentimentality was lost in favour of the practical side of running a factory. Although there was a redundancy cheque, that doesn't replace the regular pay packet coming in every week in every year.

I think for the first time in my life I hated being 'The Boss'.

"A family business isn't just about making a living, it's a way of life. An extended family where everyone is important in making it a success."
Steve Pateman

XI

Erotica

"Do you realise how much stock we've got?" Stan's face was a picture.

Panic!

He and I were standing in the middle of the factory.
"I know. A hell of a lot!" Stan looked at me and then at our show stock.

The small area that we had 'mocked up' to resemble our Olympia show stand in the factory was at bursting point and we still hadn't managed to fit all of the stock in.

How could we know which would be the best sellers and which wouldn't? We just had to take a gamble and hope we'd got it right. We decided that we'd take what we thought would sell, and if something in the catalogue was called for that we hadn't brought, we'd take the order and the cash and send it as soon as possible after the show.

Our stand, at eighty square metres was to be our office, our shop, our home and our future all in one! When I realised how much stock we had I wondered where on earth we were going to put it.
"What are we going to do?" Stan was obviously on the same wave-length, "we'll have to find somewhere else for the rest."

What else could we do? We were taking boots and shoes in each design in eleven sizes, 3 to 13, in a variety of colours, in leather and PVC, all in boxes. Not just one pair of each, we had to be ready to sell two, three, goodness knows how many pairs of the popular sizes.

We'd also brought clothes and accessories and to add to our problem we'd have to find room for the boxes of catalogues that were due to be delivered to the show.

"I'm going to see if the organisers have an area we can use as a stock room." It was the only answer. Stan agreed. I went off to make a few phone calls. Fortunately, they did have an old store room that wasn't being used. Another problem solved.

That was all very well, but the room was on the other side of the hall and if someone wanted something that wasn't on the stand, one of us would have to run across and get it.

The other thing we had to organise was how we actually kept a record of the stock we were selling and the stock that remained.

Just as we solved one problem, another one seemed to raise its ugly head. With no stock control, barcodes and so on, it would be down to good old fashioned stock-taking with loads of sheets of paper and pens.

We hired a seven-and-a-half-ton box lorry that we loaded with our equipment, our stock and our hopes, then left for London on the Thursday. As we manoeuvred the truck through the early morning rush hour we eventually arrived at Olympia, the venue for the Erotica Show. It was to be our home for the next five days; a day to set up, three days of the show and a day to pack up.

The truck had to be unloaded and the two of us had to carry everything the five hundred metres from the vehicle to our allocated stand space. Stan and I were hard at work when over the tannoy came a message, "Divine Footwear; please make your way to the loading bay as you have a delivery".

Our new catalogues had arrived! Boxes upon boxes. We ripped open the top box and there it was, the catalogue; our pride and joy. There were the glossy pages with the full colour photographs, the huge range of boots and shoes as well as all the other products we were selling. Tucked inside each catalogue was a white, printed, paper insert giving the prices with codes for each item.

Stan grabbed a copy, "Oh my God! Have you seen this Steve?" I hadn't. He passed me the white paper insert. The prices were all wrong. "These are the wholesale prices. What are we gonna do? We've got no retail prices."

Ten thousand price lists all useless and in less than twenty-four hours the doors would be opening. I got on the phone to the printers. It was their mistake and they apologised. They just couldn't understand what had gone wrong.They promised to put it right and get the new price list to us as soon as possible.

Luckily, we had a couple of copies of the correct retail prices so we would have to use those for Friday, the first day of trading. This would make even more work for us as we'd have to keep referring to the list. Pretty soon we would get to know the prices off by heart!

All these minor, and some major, hitches served to remind us that we were absolutely green behind the ears. Düsseldorf was one thing; there we took samples and orders for potential clients; here we had stock to sell to eager customers. We were selling to the general public who knew what they wanted…and wanted it now!

The show was unreal; it was big, bold, outrageous and loud. I was determined that as soon as the doors opened, people would be drawn to our stand. We had big banners designed so that we could be seen from a distance. We had metal frames made for us to hang the 'Divine' signs on.

We had Jane and another model to help show off our ranges as well as a few friends, family and my long-suffering wife who said they'd help out.

It was all about image. We put on a real show; I wanted it to look like a nightclub with music, flashing lights and a smoke machine. We certainly made sure the customers knew we were there! But would it be enough? We were the new kids on the block. Would we be accepted?

Friday, the first day of trading was absolutely manic; mayhem, unreal, but brilliant. Our goods apparently were just what our customers wanted. They loved our designs, materials, quality and the fitting; but above all, if we hadn't taken enough stock we could promise delivery within weeks, not months like some of our competitors.

That night after the doors closed we were exhausted. Our first day had been so busy and we'd sold far more than we ever thought we would.

We took five minutes to relax and have a drink and then we looked round. The stand was littered with evidence of the day's incredible trading. Odd boots and shoes, leather thongs, hand-cuffs, catalogues, Coke tins, sandwich wrappers, the place was like a 'Kinky' war zone!!

I started to set to and clear up while Stan tackled the cashing up and the credit card slips.

"This can't be right," he stared at the credit card machine and the slips, "I reckon the machine must have gone wrong."
 "Why, what's the matter?" I left what I was doing and went over to him. "I know we were busy," Stan said, "but I never dreamed we'd taken this much. Over five grand, and that's without the cash, I haven't even started counting that yet."

I couldn't believe it either. But we had, we'd topped £5,000 plus over £2,000 in cash on our first day. We'd still got two more days to go. All the hard work, the worry and the sleepless nights had been worth every minute.

On the Saturday morning we had to do a massive stock-take of everything ready to open for day two. Luckily the printers had come up trumps and a courier brought boxes of the reprinted price lists just in time for the opening at 12 noon.

With the BBC due at any moment, one of our friends who was helping on the stand piped up, "It may be a crazy idea but you know the bed you've got for people to sit on while they try on their boots?"

"Yes," I said, hesitating.

"Well, why don't you get Jane to take a rest and lie on the bed and do what she does best; some glamorous poses in her PVC gear and thigh-length boots?"

I thought about it for a split second. "We can do crazy." It was a great idea.

The sight of Jane lying on the bed was like honey for the bees! The press and the crowds loved it. The trouble was now, there was hardly any room for the customers especially with the BBC camera crew filming us. Jane was enjoying every moment; she was in her element!

In one of our rare quiet moments when we were catching our breath, a voice whispered in my ear, "Can I sit on it?" a glamorous woman asked looking at the bed and holding a pair of thigh-length boots. "Of course," I said. "Sit down, take the weight off your feet and try the boots on."

"Could you help me? I simply can't do a thing with these nails," she purred wiggling her long bright scarlet claws in the air," I've only just had them done. I'd just die if I broke one!" Her long black eyelashes fluttered in my direction.

She was beautifully made up and she was wearing a stunning outfit. As I looked closer I realised that this glamorous woman was actually going to be my first encounter with a cross-dresser. The BBC spotted this slightly awkward situation and, with her permission, started to film me helping her into the boots.

It was something very different for me, I'd never actually fitted a cross-dresser before. I'd zipped myself into boots for the photo shoot, but this was a bit of a challenge. I'm a bloke, he was a bloke and I was helping her to put on a pair of thigh-length boots with four-and-a-half inch heels for the first time. I wanted to be professional. I thought to myself, "Just don't get embarrassed, and especially, DON'T GO RED!!"

Now you may wonder what the big deal was, I'd zipped Jane into her boots many a time, but this was different. As my hand pulled the zipper up higher and higher, suddenly there was something in the way! Something that Jane didn't have, if you follow my meaning!

"Oh, you're so right, they do go up all the way…careful!" She said with a knowing grin. Curses! My face flushed scarlet with burning embarrassment yet again. You'd think by now I'd be ready for anything, but obviously, I was still learning!

Anyway, with a bit of manoeuvring we got the boots on and she turned to me and, as though it was scripted, she said, "Oh, these are absolutely Divine darling, wonderful, absolutely Divine." At this point, we knew we'd chosen the right name. She turned to the camera, flicked the hair from her face and in the softest, sexiest voice she purred into the camera, "I'm such a tart, for me nothing less than four and a half inches will do!"

We laughed. It was the next best thing to a Royal Warrant; she alone could have sold our merchandise!

Erotica was everything I hoped it would be. It gave the BBC something unique to film, a whole new world; people being strapped to racks, people upside down on cart-wheels, others being whipped, stilt walkers, people in PVC and rubber. It was the jewel in the crown for them.

All the customers were trying on and buying footwear and clothes. The cross dressers and the lap dancers were all happy to be filmed and what's more, tell the world about 'Divine'. It was more than we could ever have hoped for.

What made it for me was that we were meeting such a wide variety of people. Boyfriend and girlfriend, boyfriend and boyfriend, girlfriend and girlfriend and then there were the threesomes, the foursomes and the swingers; they were all picking items of clothing not only for themselves but also for their partners. My eyes were opened. All of a sudden sex wasn't as simple as I was led to believe!

The important thing was that they were real people who were just so genuine; so open and honest with their opinions. They wore their hearts on their sleeves and what's more, they were so comfortable in their own bodies, whether they be large or small; they just wanted to have fun.

I instantly warmed to these people, none of whom I would have met in any other situation; they were like a breath of fresh air, no pretence, no secrets amongst themselves and what's more they seemed to warm to us, take us under their wing and show us the ropes. They seemed more like friends than customers.

We were a huge success. Having the BBC there made us even more so, and when the word got round that there were cameras rolling, the crowds came flocking.

The fabulous, outrageously dressed customers loved the attention and instantly put on an impromptu show, playing to the cameras.

We were at the forefront of our field. There were a couple of other stands selling similar things, mostly imported, and they weren't doing their marketing the way we were.

What was so incredible was that the stall-holders who up to then had been our competition, even came to the stand when the cameras were off to talk to us. Clearly they loved our products and they welcomed us into their world! We got on really well because they knew we had done everything independently. After all, we were now part of the same scene.

We could learn from each other and I for one, realised that some of their products could be used for our next catalogue. If they were willing to deal with me, and they were more than welcome to buy stock, wholesale, from me.

Who could believe it, we were now networking with the best in our new-found business enterprise.

Michele and the BBC crew agreed it was the Erotica show that made the programme and it was also what made 'Divine'. From being unknown in this new industry, we were hyped up to one of the leading lights. 'Divine' had become a brand. Everybody knew our name. The Kinky Boot factory had made it and was now firmly on the map. Our Kinky Boots had become a reality.

"When zipping up thigh boots, a finger behind the zip is a must! Trust me!!!"
Steve Pateman

XII

A Cut Above the Rest!

After 90 long hours of recorded tape Michele and her team ended up with a 40-minute programme, 'Trouble At The Top'.

"How the hell can you take out the relevant bits from all that filming?" I was amazed and intrigued.

"Well, my aim was to do justice to the story." Michele looked me straight in the eye. "All through filming I had a pretty clear idea of what I wanted as the final product. A small village location, a 115-year-old business, a family man, a boss, a traditional company and a community coming to terms with Kinky Boots."

She certainly seemed to have it all planned and how she wanted it to look.

"It's a business programme," she continued, "I wanted to show how a struggling business took such risks to survive. And come on, Steve; a boss who's prepared to shave his legs and do the modelling himself? That's got to be a winner!"

We both laughed.

She went on, "You are a boss who did things he'd never done before and went to places that he never knew existed; the gay clubs, the fetish clubs, the swingers' clubs and the Erotica Show! You were prepared to do things that would make most bosses curl up and die. And of course, it had that sexy element and sex always sells. It'll be great, trust me."

I felt a little humble. She was right, I had thrown myself in 'lock, stock and barrel' and I had done things and visited places that normally I'd never have visited in a million years. It was clear that she wanted her business programme to show the serious side, but also to have that fun side too. I was really pleased but apprehensive that she was so happy with the end product.

The programme was to be called 'The Kinky Boot Factory'; that's what my employees had now renamed us!! Even the villagers referred to us now as The Kinky Boot Factory and not Brookes. It was to be broadcast at 9.50pm on Wednesday 24th February 1999 on BBC2. It was not exactly what you'd call peak time, midweek, in the winter, on the channel that only the serious viewers watched!

Out of the six programmes in the series we were to be number three. As I mentioned earlier, their first programme was to be that big, highly publicised, heavily trailed show, intended to attract huge audience figures. Yes, it was about the launch of Vogue Magazine in Russia. Yes, it was to be a glossy, big budget launch in St Peter's Square and the Russian slant was good, but would it secure their biggest audience ever?

As the editing of 'The Kinky Boot Factory' went on, the editing team along, with Michele, suddenly realised what they'd actually got. They were all in hysterics while they were working on it. They were laughing, they were crying, they were oooing and aaahing in all the right places. They felt sorry for us, they were excited with us; it had all the emotions that made a successful show. It was then that they decided that this was more than a business programme; it was going to appeal to loads of people.

"Steve, we've had a wonderful time editing and, having seen the finished show, we reckon it's something a bit special." Michele phoned me one morning out of the blue. As soon as I heard her say "Hello Steve", I knew she had something important to say, I could hear it in her voice. "So I've spoken to the Editor of the Series, Robert Thirkell, and we've decided your programme should go out as number two."

"Second, fourth, sixth, it's all the same to me really, I'm just happy that we've done a good job and the factory's come out well." I meant it. I didn't care when or where it went out. I was going to be just as embarrassed whenever it was shown.

So number two it was. We carried on making shoes and boots and getting on with our mail order customers, trying to keep our business side going as well as fulfilling the orders we'd taken from Düsseldorf. Then all of a sudden I had another call from Michele.

"Steve, we've really got a bit of a coup. We've got Robert Lindsay to do the voice-over."
"Robert Lindsay, who? Robert Lindsay the famous actor? Citizen Smith? Wolfie from years ago?" I wasn't expecting that.
"Oh yea, yea. Have you heard of him?"
"Heard of him? I've met him."

It was quite strange. It was true. Back in my teenage days spent with All Hallows Youth Club, I actually went down to see him filming one of the first episodes of 'Citizen Smith'.

"Oh wow, well if you have a chance to talk to him, tell him that I'm the guy who came to see him many years ago." I laughed.

"That's a great little story", Michele said with her tongue firmly in her cheek. I knew it was never going to go any further than that.

Then she rang me back about a week later just to give me an update as she did quite often.

"Steve, I've got great news."
I said, "Oh yes, what's happened?"
"We've had another rethink. You're not going to be number two in the series, you're going to be number one."
"Oh OK." She must have been disappointed at my reply.
"You don't sound very pleased."

I said, "Well I said before, number six, number, four, number one, it's still going out on the telly. What's the big deal?"

"Well, number one is the launch programme."
"But it's not the first series, is it? It's the second." I still couldn't see what was so special.
"Don't you see. All the publicity, the hype, the build-up. The attention from the press."

I said, "Oh OK, it's only going to be a couple of lines and a photo. It's not going to be much."

She said, "No, no, seriously, it really changes things. The thing is, while we were doing the voice-over with Robert Lindsay, he was reading the scripts to the video on the screen and half way through he said, 'That's it. I'm sorry, I'm not doing this any more.'

We all looked round, we were quite shocked. We wondered if we'd offended him or something. We asked him if there was a problem. He said, 'I can't do this programme any justice. I've got to see what Steve and his crew get up to. I need to see the end. I can't do the right voice, the right intonation unless I know where we're going with the story. This is gold.' That was a relief, I can tell you!"

Michele was so excited as she told me all this. "So on the strength of his recommendation and his enthusiasm, we're putting you as the first programme."
I said, "Oh! OK I understand, but what sort of press and publicity are we talking about?"
"Steve, you are going to be really, really busy. There'll be lots of interviews and photo shoots; you're going have to come to London…"

I interrupted her, "Oh, it's not going to be that much, it's a business programme for goodness sake, BBC2 at 9.50 on a Wednesday. Not many people are going to watch it." As I spoke, I could feel her frustration oozing out of the phone. I was convinced she was building me up only for me to be bitterly disappointed later.

"Steve. Listen. This programme has sparked so much interest. The Controllers have seen some clips from it and they're just jumping around like excited school children."

The conversation ended and I got back to my daily routine and thought little more of it.

A couple of days later she phoned again.
"It's all confirmed; your number one."
"Oh OK."
"You're still not convinced are you?" She sighed.
"Michele, this is only a factory. This is just a new product line. At the end of the day I'm here to sell shoes and that's what I'm doing."

She was still determined that I was going to understand, "And this is what we're doing. We've got a dedicated team in the office who'll be running your show. You've got a Press Officer and there'll be somebody who'll be monitoring everything that comes in. We don't want you to answer any press calls until you've cleared it with us."

I thought it was still a bit of over-kill. I envisaged the local paper sending a part-time reporter with a cameraman, or at most the local TV coming from Norwich to do a two-minute slot. But how wrong I was.

The BBC sent out press packs to everybody. Papers, TV companies, Radio producers, you name it. Cards with the details of the transmission date and a picture of me kneeling down in red ankle boots were printed and sent out. They'd sold it as 'Shaving his legs and learning to walk in six-inch stiletto heels are just two of the things Steve Pateman is doing to save his family business'.

"We've made a trailer and it'll be going out at regular intervals to promote the series." Michele's words were to ring in my ears for days to come. And then…

I'd not been home long from work. Sara and I got our son Daniel ready for bed and we sat down to have something to eat in front of the telly.

The six o'clock news had told us what was happening in the world and suddenly I heard music come on and I glanced up and there was a picture of me staring back at me. That was the first time that all Michele's big build up really hit me.

Sara and I sat open mouthed. We looked at each other. Then back at the TV, then back at each other. "Oh Hell!" we both exclaimed simultaneously. There was me in boots. There was Jane. There were Sara and Daniel. There was the Kinky Boot Factory. All on the telly.

"I bet no one was watching at this time of day." Who was I trying to convince?
"Don't be too sure." Sara was far more realistic than I.

Within seconds the phone rang. And it rang all night. It started with my parents, and then friends and then other people phoning to say "Ay-up Kinky Boots." We had neighbours knocking at the door, "You kept that bloody quiet, didn't you? Come on, tell us the story."

The power of the BBC hit me for the first time. It was all going to intrude on my life, our lives. I really thought it was going to be low key, even something that people would forget once it had gone out. And here it was starting already. If a thirty-second trailer had this effect what would happen after the programme was broadcast? A cold chill of reality started to creep over me. I was soon to find out.

Following the programme trailer giving a glimpse of my new world of business, I was in demand. Every day journalists, photographers and film crews, having been cleared by the BBC, were knocking on my door.

The national newspapers, the cultural magazines, the TV listing guides, they either interviewed me over the phone or came to the factory. My shaved legs, high-heeled shoes and boots were hot stuff. For a week or so I was constantly in and out of heels.

A week or two later Sara and I were invited to Shepherd's Bush to watch a preview of the programme before it was broadcast. Michele met us at Reception and took us on a guided tour. We felt like real celebrities as an entourage accompanied us around the building.

I arranged that, since we were in London, I'd take the opportunity to go and see a couple of customers. So I'd brought my big suitcase full of samples. The suitcase was the same one with the squeaky wheels that I always used.

One of the entourage laughed, pointed at the case as I dragged it behind me, "Those wheels really do squeak. I thought it was a prop for the programme, a bit of window dressing," she laughed, "I'm sure the BBC could lend you some WD4o!"

We were on our way to the BBC Staff Restaurant to have something to eat before the showing. There were long echoing corridors everywhere and I didn't notice it, but my suitcase must have sounded dreadful, squeaking and grinding along the hard tiled floors.

Anyway, this guy came towards me and he looked at the squeaking suitcase, "That's not annoying is it?" I hadn't got a clue who he was although he looked vaguely familiar, but Sara's pretty well up on famous people.

"You know who that was, don't you?"
"No, who?"
"It was Jonathan Ross."
I went, "Oh cheers mate, thank you!"
Sara said, "You really don't know who that was?
I said, "No, haven't a clue."

We had a really good meal in the canteen. I was constantly looking round.
Sara spotted me and asked, "What the hell are you doing?"
"Celeb spotting."
She laughed, "Fat chance of you spotting any celebs with your record.
You've just walked straight past Jonathan Ross!"

As it happened, that lunchtime the canteen was totally devoid of anyone famous, at least that I knew of!

Then we went off to see the screening. I expected we'd be in a big auditorium, but we ended up in Michele's office. They wheeled a TV set in and whammed a cassette in and 'Trouble at the Top – The Kinky Boot Factory' rolled.

There were quite a few of us there as well as Michele and other members of the production team. As the programme was running, we were watching the screen but they were watching me. They wanted to see my reactions. They wanted me to be happy with it. I must admit, I was!

I know it was a business programme but it was fun, real fun. I must say, there's nothing worse than watching yourself on television and hearing yourself speaking. It was like someone scraping glass with a kitchen knife. At times I wanted to curl up and die.

At the end Michele said, 'Well? What did you think?"
"It was OK, yes, it was good. But there was one bit I didn't like."
Michele looked quizzical. "Which bit?"
"I didn't like the shots outside the factory where we saw some of the employees smoking."

I'll never forget the look of relief and amusement on Michele's face. "Is that ALL?" We laughed. "Seriously, what did you really think?"

"Actually Michele, I did like it. You've shown us in a good light. There's nothing I can complain about at all. Oh I know I'm never going to live it down, the boss who shaves his legs. I'm going to be known as 'The Kinky Boot Man' from now on, but it was good."
"Oh I'm so pleased, we must have cut it and re-cut it so many times to get it right, but out of the 90 hours of tape we started with, we really feel we've cracked it."

"You have. It's everything I'd hoped for and more."

That was the sign of approval she and the team had hoped for.   Sara and I said our goodbyes and went off to my other appointments of the day. But as we were a bit early, we found a café and had a cup of coffee. We kept going over what had just happened to us. We were reliving the programme and picking it over again and again wondering how it would be accepted by my family, friends and the great British public.

"It's only a business programme; it's not going to affect us really." I said, still trying to convince, myself. "People will watch it and it'll be over. A flash in the pan! It might help us in the trade, but that's all. Who watches a BBC2 business programme anyway?"

In those days we didn't have dozens of channels to watch as we do now; most homes had BBC 1 and 2, ITV and Channel 4 and that was about it.

But perhaps if there was something a bit sexy to watch, even if it was on BBC2, would people watch it?

Would they really watch it?

"Shaving his legs and learning to walk in six-inch stiletto heels are just two of the things Steve Pateman is doing to save his family business."
Michele Kurland

XIII

The Birth of The Kinky Boot Man

So, we'd seen the programme at the BBC, we were really pleased with it. The true test was about to take place.

All of a sudden, the press releases started to appear in the national press and every TV magazine. We went out and bought them all! We collected anything and everything that mentioned Kinky Boots. The listing for Wednesday 24th February 1999 in every magazine and paper had a picture of me standing in Kinky Boots or shoes.

I was quite confident that not many people would be interested in a business documentary that was being transmitted at 9.50 on a Wednesday evening on BBC 2. I know it wasn't the sort of thing I'd want to watch normally. In many ways, because of that, I was quite relaxed.

We decided, for the fun of it, we'd invite a few friends round to our house for drinks, a snack and a chance to see me making a complete ass of myself. If we could get them all in the room at the same time, at least I could get the micky-taking over and done with all in one go.

However, that wasn't to happen. Michele called and said, "Right Steve, we need you here on the 24th. We want you to do some interviews and publicity on the day."

My heart sank. "Oh no!" I said, "Michele, I've already planned a bit of a party here so we can watch the programme with friends and family."

"Sorry Steve, we really need you here. I know you might think it's a bit of a pain, but we've lined up a couple of big interviews for you to do." Poor Michele, she sounded a bit apologetic, but clearly, she wasn't in the mood to argue. So Sara was going to have to have the party at home without me!

Wednesday 24 February 1999 - 'D-Day'! 'Trouble at the Top' was being broadcast. As usual, the BBC paid for my train ticket to London. Michele had asked me to take a model with me; Danielle volunteered as she'd helped us before and was local.

We had several interviews arranged during the day and the important one was with Simon Biagi in a 'props' store in the basement of TV Centre in Shepherd's Bush. It was a ten-minute promotion of 'Trouble at the Top' that was going out later that evening.

It involved Danielle and me parading around in our Kinky Boots doing a question and answer interview, mostly concerned with me having shaved my legs, which in those days was something pretty novel for a bloke!

The interview went well although we raised a few eyebrows with our PVC boots. All the arrangements had been made for us to stay in a small, rather inexpensive hotel just round the corner from TV Centre. It was the sort that used to be called a 'Commercial Hotel'; in other words, it was for drivers, reps and salesmen who needed a cheap bed for the night in London.

We booked in at Reception. "I hope you'll be comfortable." The man behind the counter said as he handed us our keys.
There was one important question I had to ask. "Are there televisions in the rooms?"
He looked apologetic and said, "'Sorry, I'm afraid not. There's one in the lounge."
"Is there any chance I could, sort of, book it for tonight?" I knew it was an odd request, but apart from anything else, I wanted Danielle to see the show. "I don't see why not," the bloke replied, "why? Is there something special on?"

A tad embarrassed, I said, "Well, yes, it's a programme about me!"
"Ooo! I say! I might pop in to watch if I get a chance." His face lit up as he spoke. "We've only got a few men staying tonight. I think they're all going out so you should have it all to yourselves!"

Great! I was pleased to have that sorted out. We took our things up to our rooms and Michele arrived to take us off for a meal and to do another interview. This was for radio, so it shouldn't take quite so long and it would certainly be less stressful. At least, that's what I thought.

It turned out that we weren't going to a studio; it was a 'live' interview, we'd be doing it either during or after the meal depending on the time slots in the programme and I'd be doing it by mobile phone.

The restaurant was very good, Italian and obviously popular. It had a super atmosphere and was buzzing with quite a few customers who were eating, drinking and having a great time.

Luckily we had finished the meal when Michele handed me her mobile phone. "Here you are, they've just rung and told me you'll be on shortly," she said, "you'll have to go and find somewhere quiet before they ring you."

"What, in here?" I couldn't believe it, "Here in the restaurant?" I said, "It's a bit noisy."

"Try the loo." She laughed.

It was a very small Italian restaurant in the heart of Shepherds Bush and, by now, it was getting busier. Perhaps it might have to be the Gents, if I couldn't find anywhere else.

So I stood in the little passage area between the Gents and the Ladies', waiting for the phone to ring. That was no good; it was way too noisy and way too public. A couple of young women came past, chattering. I needed to get away from the noise. There was no option, so I just had to go into the Gents proper! There was a bloke already in there and a split second later the door swung open and another chap came in.

The phone rang! I had to answer it, after all it was a 'live' interview. "Oh no! Sorry," I said speaking into space! "sorry, I'm trying to find somewhere quiet, can you hear me?"

The two heads half turned round towards me. They didn't care; they had other things on their minds. I heard a voice on the end of the phone. "Is that Steve Pateman?"
"Yes, yes, I'm here." I said, hoping the men would hurry up and go.
"Great." Said the voice. "Let's just set the levels. "What did you have for breakfast?" I remembered that's what interviewers always like to ask to take a sound level check.
"Corn flakes and toast." I said with my hand cupped over the phone.

The two men spun their heads round, staring and glaring at me, wondering what the hell I was on about. They, of course, had no idea I was answering questions, they were only hearing one side of the conversation. Then the interview started…

"Oh yes, I had to I shave my legs." As I spoke, I felt my face falling into a kind of grimace as though I was giving up all hope!

The quick-fire questions kept coming, and so did my answers,
"Yes I modelled the Kinky Boots."
"Yes, in PVC, leather, leopard print materials."
"Yes, in thigh length boots with four-and-a-half inch stilettos."
"Of course I enjoyed it, I loved it."

My new-found audience of two, looked at each other, then back at me and, united in disgust, headed for the door. I could only imagine what they were thinking. As they hurried out, one of them sneered, "Get a life you pervert! Can't you have your filthy chats somewhere more private?"

I just smiled as the faceless voice on the phone asked me more questions. The interview went well. It was good. Surreal, but good.

My progress back to Michele and Danielle was like running the gauntlet. I felt all eyes were on me. I wondered whether the two blokes who'd unwittingly overheard my entirely innocent one-sided conversation had shared their experience with the rest of their table?

"Don't ever ask me to do that again." I pretended to be livid with Michele, "Those blokes over there in the corner think I'm the biggest 'perv' in London after hearing my one-sided interview!"

"Well, they stayed to listen, didn't they?" I could see she was really enjoying this.

We said our 'Good byes', Michele put us in a taxi and we went back to our hotel. It was almost nine thirty.

We stood in Reception and I turned to Danielle, "Do you want to go to your room, or are you OK?"
"No, I'm fine." She replied.

We looked round to see which way to go. There was a sign with one nail holding it at one end. It had slipped and was pointing to the floor. It said, 'Lounge'. We glanced at it and laughed. We went towards the lounge door and opened it.

"Oh no!" I gasped. There were some men in the TV lounge. They weren't just men. They were half a dozen strapping great blokes. A scaffolding crew. And they were glued to the television. It was a UEFA game and they were sitting there, immersed in it.

"Oh!" I muttered again. They turned round and glared at me as though I'd walked in on a secret service conference.
"What d'yer want?" A surly scaffolder said.
I felt my voice suddenly withering. I tried to sound positive.
"I had a word with the Manager and he said…I could…watch…a programme…on…BBC2."
"We're watching the football." Growled another. "What d'yer want?"

I drew myself up to my full six-foot two. "Well' it's a programme about me actually." There, I'd said it and waited. Nothing! "It's about Kinky Boots, sex clubs and models. Danielle's one of them, and…"

Danielle slinked past me and into view of the men. It may have had something to do with her long legs, mini skirt and tight, skimpy top. "Hi boys." She said, tossing her long hair over her shoulder.
Immediately, like a rat up a drain-pipe, Boss Scaffolder leapt up and pressed a button on the TV. "You did say BBC 2 didn't you?"

The other men fought each other to make a space for Danielle to squeeze onto a sofa. From that moment, we had them in the palms of our hands!

Then it started. 'Trouble At The Top'. My programme. My story. And what did I do? I spent the next forty minutes, not watching the telly, but watching the faces of the six burly blokes. They were captivated. They laughed, they oo'd and aaah'd, they grimaced at my embarrassing moments. But what were they really thinking?

The credits rolled up and the programme came to an end. What had they made of it? Would they let me out alive? I soon found out.

The big, burly boss of the gang, tattoos all up his hairy arms, stood up in silence. He marched over to the TV set. Switched it off and turned to face me.

I was a quivering wreck. I tried to make myself as small as I could. He took a step towards me. "He's going to hit me." I thought to myself. He put out this great big gorilla-like scaffolder's hand and grabbed mine.

"Mate." He said, shaking my hand vigorously. "Bloody marvellous. How did you get involved in that? All I can say is, you've got balls!"

And that was it. We were like life-long friends. They found a few cans of beer. The questions flowed, and the guys were great.

It was quite a long session; they quizzed us about every detail.
"How did you get involved, mate?" said one.
"What about them models?" said another.
"What it was like making the programme?" chipped in a third.
"The photo shoot and the naked girls?" said the big guy.
There was a pause. Then the smartest dressed piped up, "What was it like actually wearing the boots?"

The others all stopped in their tracks and turned and glared at him and the big boss said, "What d'yer mean, "Wot's it like wearin' the boots?" D'yer want some then? Is there something you want to tell us?" They all had a good laugh at his expense.

We finally made our excuses and left them to it and went upstairs.

As Danielle went to her room I said, "Don't you think that was weird?"
She turned and agreed, "Weird's not the word. I never expected that sort of reaction from them."
"Nor did I. I wonder what other surprises we'll get. Sleep well."

We were soon to find out!

At midnight I was just creeping into bed and I decided I'd phone Sara, but she beat me to it.
"What have we done?" she said with nervous excitement in her voice.
"What d'you mean? What have we done?" I wondered if I'd committed some unforgivable crime!

"The phone has NOT stopped ringing since the credits went up on the programme. The minute I put it down, it rings again, and it's now midnight and I'm going to have to take the phone off the hook. I've got to get some sleep, I'm working tomorrow remember."

"Poor you! We never expected that reaction. Get off to bed, I'll phone in the morning, hopefully things will quieten down by then."

I eventually slept like a log, to be woken by my mobile phone. It was Sara again telling me she'd just put the phone back on the hook and it started all over again. Friends and family called, even school friends and people we hadn't seen for many years, found us in the phone book, and had rung up out of the blue just to congratulate us. Sara had now declared there and then that we'd have to go 'ex-directory', because she couldn't put up with this much longer!

I couldn't talk because Danielle and I had to catch an early train back to the unglamorous world of work! Over breakfast we were reliving the evening's unlikely events when my phone rang. It was Michele.

"What did you think?" She sounded so excited. "Did you like it?"
"Well sort of." I said without thinking.
"What do you mean, sort of?" Disappointment crept into her voice.
"Yes, we enjoyed it all right, but it turned out to be the most extraordinary evening."

I told her about our not-so-private viewing and the scaffolders and their unexpected generosity! She shared our surprise at the reaction and she couldn't wait to tell what had happened at her end.

"You won't believe it, but we've had the most incredible response here." She was bubbling like a bottle of Champagne.

"The BBC switchboard has been going mental!" she said, "People have been ringing in; they want to know more about you, where you are, asking where they can buy the gear. Have you heard anything?"

"Yes, Sara rang at midnight, she's had dozens of calls, she's vowed were going ex-directory! We're..." I couldn't finish my sentence. She burst in again.

"Hard luck, but that's the price of fame! They've told us the initial estimate of the viewing figures is well over the three million mark, isn't that fantastic?"

I said, "Oh, OK." The figure didn't mean that much to me at this stage.

"Is that good?"

"We've never had so many. We usually only take about two million viewers. That's without the final figures. The total might be even higher."

I was still in denial! All I could keep in mind was that it was a Wednesday night, BBC2 and a business programme. I was still convinced it would have little effect on the viewing figures.

With a cheery, "I'll keep in touch." Michele rang off and we gathered our belongings and left for the tube station.

It was rush hour and London's Underground system was in full swing. Finding two seats together was a bit of a problem especially since we had rather a lot of luggage, most of it mine! I had my rucksack as well as my trusty suitcase…the one with the squeaky wheels. It had also acquired a couple of 'Divine Footwear' stickers.

All of a sudden, I had that funny feeling that someone was looking at me. The guy opposite was staring over at Danielle and me and at the stickers on my case. Being the polite country boy that I am, I said "Hi ya, how you doing?"

Most people never speak to anyone on the tube in London, unless you're a weirdo that is. So I didn't expect any reply.

"Don't I know you?" It was the man opposite. Obviously he'd made a mistake.
"No." I said dismissively and looking away. "No, I'm not from here I'm from Northamptonshire." But he was insistent.
"No, I do know you, you've been on telly haven't you?"
Danielle nudged me gently.
"I know," the man said, "you're the Kinky Boot man, aren't you?"

I said, "What?"

"Yes, that's the case with the squeaky wheels and the stickers." He said, "We saw you last night."

I had to give in and admit it.

Then he looked round the carriage and he did the unthinkable. He started talking to the person next to him and then the one on the other side and before long he was shouting to everyone. And what was he shouting? "He's the Kinky Boot Man, he was on telly last night."

Within seconds the whole carriage was alive with people saying they'd seen it too. They were reliving the programme and asking me questions. It was utterly bizarre and wonderful.

Danielle and I sat there with all this conversation going on around us. When we reached our station, we simply and calmly stood up, trying not to look too clumsy as we manhandled our luggage. We turned and said to the assembled travelling British public, "Cheers, bye. See ya!"

"Bye Kinky Boots!" Echoed around the carriage as we all started to disperse into the anonymous morning rush-hour.

The doors closed behind us. We dropped our bags and looked at each other.

"What – on - earth just happened?" I could hardly get the words out; I was laughing so much, but now beginning to have a very uneasy feeling.
"That was unbelievable." Danielle was equally helpless.

We managed to get ourselves to the platform at St Pancras Main Line Station in good time. We agreed to have five minutes shut-eye once the train had departed. With any luck we could spend the next fifty minutes free from any intrusion, welcome or otherwise.

Still with my eyes closed, I heard the ticket collector working his way down the carriage. My wallet was in my hand ready and then suddenly: "Come on Steve, get your tickets out." I jolted up in total shock.
"What? I…" I couldn't believe it. He must be talking to someone else, surely. But no!

"Have you got your tickets, Steve?" The Conductor was talking to me and he knew my name.
"Do you know me?" I said fumbling in my wallet for our return tickets.
"Know you?" He said with a huge grin. "I know more about you than you think. You revealed it all on telly last night. You're the Kinky Boot Man."

Once again I simply couldn't believe it.

"What a laugh," he said, "Brilliant."

Then for a few minutes we had a conversation almost as though we'd known each other for years.

Off he went, checking tickets and scribbling on them with his pen as though this brief exchange had made his day.

The train pulled in to Luton. Danielle looked out of the window. "Steve. Look out there." She said giggling.

Yet again, the comedy continued. The Conductor had obviously told everyone in the carriage as he went along, and now there was a crowd of people passing, staring in, waving, giving the big 'thumbs up' and shouting at us.

As the train pulled out, my mobile phone rang. It was Dad.

"Where are you?" he yelled.
"I'm on the train. We've just left Luton." I really hate speaking on the phone on the train, so I did it in a loud whisper.
"Well you'd better get here bloody fast. The place is in chaos." He added, obviously in a state.
"Oh, hell, what's gone wrong?" I said, beginning to panic.

"We came in this morning and the fax machine had run out of paper. There's faxes strewn all over the floor, the phones are going ballistic, every time someone rings they're asking for a catalogue, we've done nothing so far this morning, apart from fend off your new customers."

So by the time I got back to Wellingborough station and then to the factory, I was shaking like a leaf.

The office was filled with fax paper. "Look at all this," Dad said pointing to the piles of paper, "a pile here, another here, all with orders or enquiries. We've had to change the paper roll on the fax machine three times! We've had to send out to get some more."

We hadn't realised how determined people were to reach us. We found out later that they'd been bombarding Directory Enquiries who were getting overloaded with callers. Other people had freeze-framed the TV film just to find out where we were.

There was even another company in Northampton called 'Brooks Books' and people were calling them in desperation. Thankfully they were quite amused and were redirecting callers to our number. It really was crazy.

Over the next week or so, the calls and faxes calmed down, but we were still getting loads of letters, not only for orders and catalogues, but surprisingly, from other small businesses all over the country, that were in the same position, struggling for survival.

Some letters congratulated me on the successful programme and others told me what troubles they were facing. Letters came from all sorts of businesses large and small, manufacturers, family firms, you name it; the programme seemed to have struck a chord with so many.

People also sent flowers, chocolates and congratulation cards. We couldn't believe the effect that we'd obviously had. Even the Mayor of Wellingborough sent us a letter of congratulations.

The general reaction to the programme was that it had hit home to so many people. The fact that we had tried to fight the odds and fly in the face of the inevitable, it seemed to inspire and give courage to others to try something new.

It was immensely moving and humbling…and surreal. Of all the hundreds and hundreds of letters, cards, emails, faxes and calls we received we never had a negative comment. The public had taken us to their hearts. The Kinky Boot factory had finally been accepted and with the help of the BBC it gave us credibility and a seal of approval.

"Kinky Boots" and "The Kinky Boot Factory" had arrived.

Not only that, I had now earned myself a new nickname, "The Kinky Boot Man".

"Men in thigh boots should be as acceptable as men in waders!"
Steve Pateman

XIV

Stepping Out in Kinky Boots!

In 1961 a new series hit the TV screens. It was called 'The Avengers' and starred Ian Hendry as Dr. David Keel aided by Patrick MacNee as John Steed. It was an immediate success and over the next eight years it proved a hit in 90 countries worldwide.

Perhaps the biggest change to the programme came in 1964 when Ian Hendry left after the first series and Patrick McNee became the leading character. Then in the second series his side-kick was Honor Blackman as Dr Catherine Gale. She was already an established actress. In fact, she was quite a star and she remained his main support until the end of the third series when she left to make the Bond movie, 'Goldfinger'.

It was the revolutionary image of Cathy Gale/Honor Blackman in black leather and long black leather boots that made her such an iconic creation. Black leather was given a life of its own as a fashion statement, and the boots became an object of desire.

Patrick MacNee and Honor Blackman even released a record with a title that introduced a new term to the language, 'Kinky Boots'. Initially released in 1964 it made no impression at all but on its re-release in 1990 it reached number 5 in the British Top Ten and stayed there for seven weeks.

So Kinky Boots had already existed and as a kid, I used to watch 'The Avengers'. Perhaps, the thought of Cathy Gale in her long black boots must have implanted itself deep down in my subconscious.

My 'Divine' range of footwear, thanks to a member of my workforce, had been labelled 'Kinky Boots' and it stuck. Then after the BBC television documentary I was called The Kinky Boot Man.

I loved the nickname and the celebrity it brought me. Wherever I went people seemed to recognise me from the TV programme. They wanted to know about the boots, the company and also about me. For a while, I suppose, I was a minor 'celeb'. It didn't stop with people in the street though. I remember once I was in a bar queuing for a drink when the barman looked over everyone else's heads and shouted, "Hey 'Mr Kinky Boot Man' what'll you have?"

I must admit it caught me by surprise and I was a bit embarrassed, even more so when he shouted to the assembled drinkers, "Hey everybody, 'Mr Kinky Boots' is in the house."

As much as I enjoyed being recognised, it has two sides to it. It's a wonderful feeling initially but as much as you want to be known, the next thing is, you don't want to be known.

Naturally, in my home village of Earls Barton and throughout the County of Northamptonshire I was something of an overnight sensation. All the local papers and journals featured articles about the factory and my story. The two local television stations, BBC East and ITV Anglia came and filmed, and I was interviewed on the BBC and commercial local radio stations. I even featured in Earls Barton Parish Magazine!

Real celebrities have it far worse than I ever did. They relish in their immense fame and when they fall from favour their demons come out. They do stupid things like guesting on terrible 'B rated' quiz shows, or they go off to the jungle in a vain attempt to rebuild their careers. Celebrity status is a very fickle friend; you're only as good as your last PR success.

For me, too much recognition meant I always had to talk about the Kinky Boots, the business, shaving my legs and about myself. I felt as though I was bragging which made me feel rather uncomfortable. Nowadays after so long, I don't mind so much and I'm quite happy if people ask, "Don't I know you from somewhere?" Now it feels good to be recognised, I love to tell the stories, but still have the guilty 'name dropping' feeling all over again!

It was as a result of the TV programme and my new found 'fame' that a new, and now very busy, side of my life developed; that of after dinner speaking.

You'd be surprised at the wide range of clubs and societies that wanted me to speak to them and I was even invited to universities and colleges to give lectures on my life as a business innovator.

My first engagement came about under a certain amount of duress!

I belonged to the Wellingborough branch of 'Round Table'. It was originally an English, now an international, all-male organisation similar in many ways to 'Rotary International', aimed at the 18 to 40 age group. As well as weekly meetings and social events they do a lot of fund raising for local communities, charities and worthy causes.

Mike, a fellow member, had moved to Essex and he phoned me one day and said, "Steve, I need a favour from you. We're looking for a guest speaker for our next dinner. We need a celebrity and I thought of you."

I said, "First of all, I'm not a celebrity; second, I've never done an after-dinner speech in my entire life and third, what the hell can I talk about?"

"What do you mean?" he shouted down the phone, "haven't you just been on the television? Everybody's been talking about you and your Kinky Boots! And anyway, we've been let down by our speaker and you're the only one I could think of who might do it. We'll pay you!"

"I really don't think it's me," I bleated, "I don't think I could do it justice, I'm not a public speaker."
"Oh come on, at our meetings you never shut up; our guys would love to hear the stories you tell," he insisted, "bring a model in slinky boots and that'll keep them happy."
"Let me give it some thought and I'll come back to you." I said stalling for time, but I was pretty sure I had no intention of doing it in a month of Sundays.

I did give it some serious thought, and gradually I came round to the idea. He was a mate and anyway, apart from him, I wouldn't know anyone in the audience so if I really messed up, I could slink away and I need never see any of them again.

Then came a second call from Mike. He really was desperate, I felt I had no choice. I reluctantly had to agree.

The day arrived. I'd asked Katy Ann Day, a local model who'd done some modelling with us if she'd be up for an unusual public appearance with dinner thrown in! She'd been a 'Page Three Girl', and said she loved doing that kind of thing. So we drove down to Essex in the late afternoon.

The venue was a four star hotel where two single rooms had been booked for us. We changed ready for a few drinks prior to dinner. I was dressed in a blazer and tie and she was, in fairness, undressed in a hot pink skimpy dress and sexy shoes.

I'd made a load of notes with bullet points to help me through and if I dried up, I'd also written the whole talk out as a back-up if all else failed. Meanwhile, Katy Ann could pose and walk around as a distraction to keep the poor old men awake and the attention off me!

Mike was Master of Ceremonies and after the initial opening speeches and notices, we started dinner. By 8.30 we'd only just had our starter, the beer was going down quickly, the men in the audience were getting more and more light headed and the butterflies in my stomach were getting more and more violent!

I was due to speak at 9.30 and they hadn't even cleared the tables from dessert. I turned to Mike and pleaded, "When am I on? They're all getting as drunk as skunks, shouldn't we have coffee and a 'comfort break'?"

"Don't worry, OK we'll have a pee break and we can have coffee while you're speaking. It'll be all right. You'll slay them."

With that he stood up, shouted, "Quiet." and banged his pint glass firmly on the table. He didn't know his own strength; the glass shattered into a thousand pieces, shards everywhere and the last dregs of beer dribbled all down his jacket.

Hotel staff rushed to his aid to clear the broken glass while members of the audience staggered out to the bar and the toilets. Mike sat with glazed eyes, still holding the handle; all that was left of his pint glass.

Eventually everyone was seated once again, the tables were cleared and the servers had provided coffee for all. Mike was in no state to introduce me, so I stood up for my debut as a speaker.

Under my trousers I was wearing my rugby shorts and unseen by anyone I'd slipped out of my trousers and pulled on my leopard skin thigh length boots under the table. I thought it would act as an 'ice breaker', so I walked round so that everyone could see what I was wearing which caused a gasp or two and few wolf whistles.

I noticed that at the back of the room there were two or three tables where mostly drunken diners were still drinking heavily, while at the front were tables with rather more mature men who were clearly determined to hang on my every word. These became my core audience.

The talk started hesitantly, but as I gained more confidence it began to flow rather well. Then mid-sentence, I had to stop.

A guy from the bar walked in, completely ignored me, and without so much as a by your leave, stood in the middle of the dining area and shouted at the top of his voice, "Last orders. Last orders at the bar." And walked out again!

At which point, a rugby scrum of inebriated diners surged towards the door, even the glamorous and sexy poses from Katy Ann Day couldn't hold back the tide. I was left with two tables of loyal listeners as I attempted to finish my talk. That was my first introduction to public speaking.

To my amazement, the guys at the front applauded keenly when I finished and agreed that I'd done a brilliant job under somewhat difficult circumstances.

Clearly they loved the story and several of them asked, there and then, if I'd come to their branches of Round Table to give a talk. From then, by word of mouth, I went round the country delivering my cheerful, usually uninterrupted, talk about Kinky Boots.

Gradually the men in 'Table' told their wives who have an all-female club called 'Ladies Circle', before long, Rotary, Inner Wheel, Women's Institute, Mothers' Union and a host of other groups heard about me and invited me along to speak.

Public speaking became easier and more enjoyable with every talk I gave, I never had to resort to making feeble jokes because the situations I described were amusing enough. After all, there's nothing funnier than real life.

As well as to groups, I've spoken in Westminster Hall, been on question and answer panels with famous people and appeared in the academic world at universities, colleges and schools, each of which had bought the 'Trouble At The Top' BBC video and used it as a teaching aid.

Even my son Dan's school used the video every year as a teaching aid for their business studies class. When the programme was recorded, it showed Dan as a two-year old toddler running around holding his cuddly toy. Each year when the video was shown and Dan was progressing through the school, "Baby Daniel" had the mickey taken out of him, which worked until he was a six foot five second-row rugby forward and all of a sudden the mickey-taking stopped!!!

I was even asked to go to Spain to address a conference of the Federación de Industrias del Calzado Españo, (the Spanish Footwear Federation) where my words were simultaneously translated into Spanish even though some of the audience spoke a little English.

Unfortunately, as the other speakers had over-run, the translator turned to me and said in her best English, "I have to leave by 5 pm to catch my flight, so you'll have to reduce the length of your talk by fifteen minutes otherwise the last part won't be translated." This left me desperately trying to cut my talk to match her early departure.

It was the most difficult speech I'd ever delivered, because as the speech was being translated into Spanish there was a natural time delay. This normally isn't a problem, but because my talk relied on lots of funny moments that (hopefully) caused laughter, as I delivered the punch line there was a stony silence, so flustered I would rush headlong into the next story. Then all of a sudden, after ten seconds or so the translator would deliver the punch line.

There's nothing more confusing and embarrassing than laughter in the wrong place. So after a while you soon realise that your talk has to go at the same pace as the speed of the translator.

Apart from all these talks I was also invited to another entirely new section of the general public; in particular, the more private sexy side, the swingers clubs.

One of our customers, who used to go to a swingers club somewhere near London, came to the factory to buy boots.
"You know, Steve, you ought to come to our club," he said, "they'd love to hear your story."
"Perhaps not, I don't know anything about swinger's clubs," I said feebly, "I don't know where they are."
"Everywhere," he offered quickly, "they're everywhere, I bet every town has a swinger's club."

Wow! That was something I'd never thought about, but if they were used by people who bought our boots and shoes, well, this was another avenue I ought to explore.

"They'd love to talk to you, get to know you and find out about the footwear, so bring along some catalogues and samples and do a table-top display. We're a really sociable crowd." He was quite persuasive.

I agreed and was duly invited along to the club. Discretion is paramount. Obviously, anyone going to a swinger's club has to respect the privacy of all other participants. Some are professionals with important jobs and their presence, if it happened to be revealed, could jeopardise their careers and their entire lives. So it was not for me to judge them. They were, just like all the other people I'd met on my amazing journey, ordinary people pursuing their particular interest.

Becoming part of such a group isn't easy. Anyone wanting to join has to be introduced by a trusted existing member, and even then, a rigorous process of checking is carried out. Without such security checks it would be easy for an under-cover reporter, for instance, to infiltrate the club and get a 'scoop' story, and that would potentially ruin many lives, careers and families.

So I turned up not having any idea of what I might find. To my relief and surprise, I met with an amazingly friendly group of people, very honest, very open and clearly, very liberated.

All preconceptions that I had were quickly pushed to one side. Far from being a free-for-all, there was a great deal of etiquette. They respected each-other, they were from all levels of society and they knew and stuck to the strict rules of behaviour. Anyone not abiding by the strict code of conduct would instantly be removed and membership revoked.

My presence there was to share information about 'Divine' products, and that is what I did. They loved the catalogues and the few items I'd brought with me. Most of them already knew about us and had already bought from us, so my job was easy.

What was most welcome for me was that they trusted me enough to share in their inner most secret lives. I have never, and would never, divulge anything about the clubs I have visited nor about its members. In return, when they ordered from us, our discretion was assured. I valued their custom and their support. They loved the fact that our company treated them with such respect.

I was subsequently invited to other swinger's clubs and met more amazingly kind and honest people. This gave me the opportunity to hear their feedback on our products and to discuss new ideas with them.

One instance was the introduction of what we called our 'ballet shoes and boots'. I imported some from Canada. They were the classic 'pointe shoes' as worn by dancers, but with a heel.

I found that many men and women were interested in these so we had to include them in our range. Mainly they were used as 'bed shoes', because not many people could walk in them! Even though I'd learned to walk in heels, these were way beyond my capabilities. Although I did wear some in a catalogue photo shoot, but I had to crawl to my posing position or sit on a stool!

Before I invested a lot of money in buying them, I visited several of the specialist clubs to see how better to improve the design.

It was a worthwhile exercise, it was product research at its absolute best because I was actually there with the people who wanted to buy and wear them.

The same experience was valuable when I was invited to visit fetish clubs. Like the swinger's clubs, these too relied on discretion and privacy. They both involved like-minded people pursuing their particular fantasies. In the case of the fetish clubs, it was very much more about the clothes and accessories we had already featured in our 'Divine' catalogues.

I quickly learned there were all sorts of levels in the fetish world; from those who simply liked wearing uniforms and heavy boots or leather clothes and our Kinky Boots, right through to the seriously 'master and slave' fetishists.

Meeting them at shows or in the specialised clubs helped me understand their needs and desires and it meant that within the 'Divine' range, we could provide exactly what they wanted.

I never dreamed I would ever be party to these eye-opening experiences. What I learned most of all was that people are people and we have no right to judge what goes on in the privacy of their own homes.

"Kinky boots bring a new meaning to dress to impress."
Steve Pateman

XV

The TV Effect!

I really thought I'd seen everything there was to see of this new world of erotica. Yet again – wrong!!

'Trouble At The Top' had 3.4 million viewers on the night, and the final figure was well over the 4 million. It had an incredible effect on our customer base. Interest came from all quarters and the surprises kept coming with numerous requests for appearances in all sorts of programmes. I was still in demand for interviews and 'The Kinky Boot Factory' was still apparently big news.

For us it was fantastic PR. The more exposure I could get for the story, the more possibilities we'd have of getting catalogues out to our potential customers.

At this time there was an explosion in the number of television channels to watch because of the onset of digital TV.

Requests for interviews started coming from some of the satellite sexy channels like 'Men and Motors' and 'Sexcetera'. Even from the 'other' channels, you know, the ones men watch in secret. "Just flicking through the channels, dear!" as their wives pass the door at an inopportune moment!

I have to say they were channels I'd never heard of, let alone, watched...'til then!!!!

Then came invitations to take part in more serious programmes. Two of the most prominent at the time were, 'The Working Lunch' a BBC business show with Adam Shaw presenting. This was followed by a request from the BBC to appear in 'The Esther Show' hosted by Esther Rantzen, a business and topical talk show that featured people with good stories to tell. Sara came with me for this one.

As they record more than one programme in a day, we were in the Green Room at Television Centre with other guests. It was then that I met a guy who was doing another show with Esther. He was Head of the British Sumo Federation and was called, what else? Steve Pateman! Luckily the producers didn't get us mixed up! I doubt that he'd have looked too hot in Kinky Boots and I certainly wouldn't have fitted the bill as a Sumo Wrestler!

As a couple of small asides, there was also another Steve Pateman who crossed my horizon, and I did get mixed up with him. He was the Chief Executive of Santander Bank and someone phoned me to ask if I'd present some business awards.

I thought it was a bit strange until it clicked and I let them down gently and told them they'd got the wrong Steve Pateman, or had they? Perhaps I could have arranged for all members of the bank staff to wear Kinky Boots!

On another occasion, Sara and I were at a local Northamptonshire car dealership looking for a new car. We sat at the desk opposite the salesman and we noticed the name-plate on his desk.

Sara nudged me as he opened the screen on his desk-top computer. She whispered, "Have you seen his name?" All I could see from where I was sitting was just 'Steve'.

"Have a look," she said, "He's got the same name as you. I can't believe it."

Then he said, "I'll just take some personal details. Can I take your name?"

With a large smile I said, "Pateman. Steve Pateman." As he started to type we could see that it was slowly sinking in. He stopped and glanced up with a questioning look on his face, "No, that's my name, sorry, I need your name."

"I know; it's mine too."

Then his face changed as he realised that he knew who I was… without knowing who I was!

"YOU?" He leaned back in his chair as it all became clear. "You've caused me so much trouble, hassle and grief since that TV programme. Talk about 'Trouble at The Top', what about 'Trouble at the car showroom'!!! My family, friends and work colleagues now call ME the Kinky Boot Man. I also live in Northamptonshire and I'm getting weird and wonderful invitations to go and tell YOUR story." He laughed.

"What's your boot size?" I joked.

"No way!" he said, "you're not getting me in any of those." I must owe the poor bloke a beer or two for the trouble I've caused him over the years.

They say, "What's in a name? I say, "Embarrassment, confusion chaos and a lot of laughs".

On the other hand, Frank, a friend of mine told me he was in a bar in London some weeks after the TV programme went out. He overhead a bloke in a crowd of women boasting, "You've probably heard of me, my name's Steve, but I'm better known as The Kinky Boot Man from the programme on the telly." A few of the group said things like, "Oh yes, I saw that," "Those boots and all those sexy outfits," "What was Erotica like?"

Frank's ears pricked up. He knew I didn't get to London that often and, anyway, the voice didn't sound like mine, so he swung round to look at 'Steve' to find a total stranger bragging to the group about his so-called celebrity status.

Being Frank he couldn't resist going over to the 'new Steve' to challenge him. "Oh, you're from Northamptonshire aren't you?"

'Steve' looked startled, "So? What of it?"

"Well, so am I! Small world isn't it? Actually, I'm from Wellingborough, just like you. Where do you live?" Frank could see the bloke starting to squirm a bit and then went in for the kill.
"I've known the family for years. Funny really, Steve's a good mate of mine." At which point the guy bolted for the door never to be seen again.

I'd often heard of people impersonating celebrities or top doctors, police, fire-fighters, but me? He must have been desperate!

Then there are the TV shows that are not really suitable for my story. One that I was invited to do was 'The Trisha Show' with Trisha Goddard for Anglia TV. She couldn't have been nicer, but the show was a little difficult for me. It was similar to 'The Jeremy Kyle Show' that digs into relationships and the conflicts within them.

Sara and her friend Sue were invited along, with my friend Andy and me. The producers wanted us to create a story line to fit in with the programme's format. That really upset us. As a professional business and we didn't want to mislead our customers.

The producers tempted us by saying the show had an average of over 700,000 viewers, mainly women, each day. Since women were our main buyers, I was foolishly tempted and I couldn't resist doing the show for that amount of exposure.

They also offered us a team of six models to show off our new Kinky Boots and 'Divine' clothing ranges.

I don't want to say too much about the ethical side of the show. Perhaps silence is, in this case, golden! But it was a massive success for the business that it generated, even though it wasn't my most successful appearance on the box!

My life had become a series of surprises! The next one came with another phone call.

"Hello, Steve?" It was a warm, friendly voice with a strong Manchester accent. "A few of us saw the programme on the telly and we were impressed. We'd like to see if we could do some business with you."

Now calls like this really make me sit up and pay attention!

She went on to tell me that she had a nationwide company that ran shops selling all the usual clothes and accessories similar to ours for cross-dressers. They also had centres where a man could go for a few hours or a day to have a complete make-over. This would involve having a new hair-do, outfit and professional make-up finished off with a photo shoot as a memento of the day.

But what they really wanted from us was to have their own branded shoes for their male and female customers. She asked if it would be something that we'd be interested in.

We went on to discuss what she wanted and her requirements were well within our capabilities; court shoes and boots, but I explained that we were anxious to keep and promote our own brand name, 'Divine'.

Nothing was settled at that stage, of course, but I did agree to travel up to Manchester to meet her and take things further. They had a shop and their headquarters in the same street.

I left for Manchester very early one morning and arrived at about 8.30, parked and walked to the address she'd given me. I quickly slipped inside as the early morning commuters were beginning to assemble at the bus stop outside.

Inside was a colourful and extensive array of merchandise. There was a woman behind the counter on the phone. She put her hand over the mouthpiece and said, "Take a seat on the sofa for a minute, I'm just talking to a customer, and then I'll be with you."

I turned and started to cross to the sofa where there were two other men sitting, just like me in suits and nursing large suitcases. I thought, "I bet theirs don't squeak like mine."

Then I was worried, I was sure I was the only one hoping to sell shoes to them. I wondered where these other two guys had come from.

For a minute it seemed like I'd got some competition. In my mind I started to go through my sales pitch; could I alter my prices? How could I make mine more competitive than theirs? All sorts of other question started to race through my mind.

After a few moments, the woman came over and whispered, "Would you like to come to the counter, so I can book you in."
So, my suitcase and I squeaked our way to the counter. "What's your name?"
"Steve Pateman." I said.
She looked at me and then at a diary, "Er, what time are you booked in for?"

"Nine o'clock appointment. Sorry, I'm a bit early." I apologised.
"There's no problem, but I can't find you in the diary." She ran her finger up and down the page.

"I should be there, "I smiled, "I have a meeting with your Managing Director. I'm Steve Pateman from Divine Footwear."
"Ah, I see the problem," she leaned forward and whispered, "You're in the wrong place, you want our Head Office, that's over the road. This our make-over centre."

Whoops! All of a sudden, the penny dropped. The guys on the sofa weren't there for the same reason at all! I was there to settle a deal; they were they for a complete make-over day. Within the hour they would be glammed up, made up, new wig, new outfit, sexy shoes and a great photo shoot.

Anyway, I swallowed my pride trying to hide my embarrassment but to no avail. Blushing and muttering apologies, I backed sheepishly out of the door.

"Thanks, bye." I threw over my shoulder as I closed the door. What an idiot! How could I get the address wrong? I knew they had a shop and their HQ in the same street. Why the hell did I go in there? I thought to myself.

I felt like dying with embarrassment. What a wally! I sighed and just about regained my composure when as I turned. There facing me was a long queue of early morning workers standing at a bus stop immediately outside the shop.

Whether it was my vivid imagination or not, I don't know, but it felt as though every single one of those commuters was staring at me, wondering what on earth I'd been up to in THAT place.

I left them wondering as I hurried across the road and found my way, this time, to the right Reception, in the right building!

The meeting went well. They wanted the court shoes with a few changes, like leather linings and so on to make them more comfy for the men who might be wearing them for longer periods, and also they wanted upgrades and higher quality leathers including patent leather.

All this we agreed on and samples were to be sent and in the end a good order was confirmed.

"Now when I get asked to a fancy dress party, my wardrobe is limitless!"
Steve Pateman

XVI

Going Dutch!

The TV programme had brought us some great customers from the UK, but it was also seen, via BBC World, in other countries too. Once again, the phone rang and yet another chapter in 'Steve's Adventures in Kinky-land' was about to unfold.

The call came from The Netherlands and it proved to be very important and very, very different. The man on the phone said he and his partner wanted to meet me; they were impressed with the programme and wanted to come over to the UK to discuss an idea they had.

They duly came and visited the factory; we showed them our complete range of Kinky products and, to my surprise and delight, they wanted the lot! Not only that, but they wanted 'exclusive' sales of 'Divine' goods for the whole of The Netherlands. What's more, they'd managed to get on board Kim Holland, one of their country's top porno stars to wear and promote our range.

I was thrilled! The chance to get our products into the 'Red Light District' in Amsterdam was just too good to miss out on. They were obviously willing to buy a huge amount of stock from us and, naturally, we'd be only too pleased to oblige!

Then came something I hadn't expected.

"So, Steve, why don't you come out to Amsterdam, then you can actually meet Kim. You can bring all your products for her to see and try on. What do you say?" His Dutch accent and winning smile certainly won me over!

"Er, yes. Why not?" What had I just said? Why don't I jump off the Niagara Falls? Why don't I swim the Atlantic? Why don't I climb Everest? There must be easier challenges!!

"We'll be doing a photo shoot and we'd like you to be part of it." He continued as I was still taking in the first shock. Then it hit me; what had he just said?
"What do you mean? You want me to be part of it? You mean…the photo shoot?" I said.

"Why not?" he added quickly, "they're your products; you're proud of them, so why not show them off? We'll pay for you to come over and give you a good time into the bargain. OK?"

Yes, why not? I swallowed extremely deeply. It was a great opportunity. I'm a grown man. I could handle anything the industry could throw at me. This was, after all, just another sales pitch. Except the very minor, teeny-weeny little fact that this one just happened to involve a number one porn star!

Then I began to ask myself if we'd hear another word about it. We'd had plenty of business leads since the TV programme that led to absolutely no orders whatsoever. On the other hand, these guys had come over to meet me and they had seen the goods and were impressed. Maybe something could come of this after all.

Two weeks later an order came through from Holland with an up-front payment. It was a big order for a load of clothing, a load of boots and shoes, some accessories as well, whips, handcuffs, rubber and PVC clothing. But they wanted me to take the products over to them in my trusty suitcase. I wondered if it would squeak in Dutch! They gave me a date to go over for the photo shoot and to meet Kim.

A flight was booked from Luton to Schiphol Airport, Amsterdam. My squeaky friend wasn't enough, so I had to have another case to accommodate all the samples, plus my clothes for the weekend. We also had to send some extra samples by carrier for the photo shoot.

At Luton my bags were weighed at check-in and they were classed as 'oversized', so I had to go to a separate desk and queue up. My turn came, and I managed to heave the first case up and put it on the conveyer belt and as it slowly moved along I put the second one next to it.

Then it struck me! With my clothes and the boots and shoes, the cases also held a collection of other items that might just set the alarms off! Hand cuffs, whips, belts with studs, big steel-capped boots along with other items of clothing with metal accessories.

The cases moved through the X-ray machine and stopped and came back and then went through again. "Phew!" I was relieved that was over. It wasn't over, it was just beginning!

The security guy picked the cases up and put them on a side table and called me over.

"Are these your cases, Sir?" He looked me straight in the eye as he spoke.

"Yes," I said hesitantly. "Is there anything wrong?"

"Can you tell me what's in them?" He had no sign of humour in his voice. Surely he'd crack once I come clean.

"Well," I said, "There are all sorts of items of metalware, buckles, belts, items of clothing and bits and pieces of props for a photo shoot that I'm doing in Amsterdam."

Already the beads of sweat were having a field day on my forehead and my whole body was pumping with my super-powered central heating system!

Then suddenly he broke out into the biggest smile you've ever seen.

"OK Steve," he laughed, "You realise why I've called you over don't you?"

I was staggered. How did he know my name? I haven't given him my passport or anything.

"Shall we open them here? What are we going to find?"

"I've told, you," I pleaded, "It's stuff for a photo shoot."

"I believe you, Steve. Don't worry. I saw you on the telly; as soon as I saw you in the queue I knew at once you were the Kinky Boot Man. These are all your samples, aren't they?"

I mumbled something inaudible.

"You can stop going red now, I've embarrassed you enough mate." He really had melted and had obviously rather enjoyed his little charade! "But next time, just declare what you're carrying, it'll save you a lot of time... and sweat!"

So the cases went through safely in one direction and off I went in another, straight to a bar for a restorative beer. It was a good flight and the bags were waiting for me at the other end with no further mishaps.

Also waiting for me at the arrivals barrier were Willem and his partner, Lenke, the couple who were going to take over the brand for The Netherlands. They had a large card bearing the word 'Divine' in big letters, so I could hardly miss them!

Before dropping me off at my hotel, they very kindly suggested we go to their home first for a drink and chat before introducing me to Kim. We arrived at their house; it was small but very smart and we sat in their lounge, had a beer and started to chat.

"I think it's time you met Kim, don't you?" Willem said.

"Oh, I thought we were going to see her later." I was a bit confused.

"Well, in person, maybe," he smiled, "but for now...!"

He moved over to a TV and pressed buttons and wow! Thank goodness I'd put my drink down on a side table or it would have been all over the furniture. On the screen was, well, how do I describe it? A full-on Dutch porno movie.

"There, you see, Steve, that beauty with the two blokes, that's Kim."
I gulped! That was my first introduction to Kim. She was everything you'd imagine a porn star to be, if you've ever imagined one, that is!

Lenke told me a bit about Kim. She had become a very good and astute businesswoman. She ran a successful contact magazine as well as a string of fetish clubs and swinger's clubs. And of course, she appeared on stage and in films as the famous Kim Holland.

Now this was all a lot to take in for an innocent lad from Barton! To top it all, they told me that the cameraman who directed all the movies and takes all her pictures, was Kim's husband. So, I'd met Kim on screen if not yet in the flesh. That was still to come.

Willem and Lenke took me to my hotel to drop off my luggage; we had something to eat and then came my tour of Amsterdam. It was my first visit and I was bowled over by what I saw. The canals, the architecture, everything was fabulous.

Finally came the other side of this beautiful city! The Red Light District. It was certainly as I had imagined it, only more so. They took me to the famous streets lined with shop windows with the young 'ladies' sitting on chairs or posing on beds selling their wares!! We paid special attention to the boots, shoes, clothes and accessories. Of course, I totally ignored the young 'ladies' in the windows. This was, after all, a business trip.

"Notice the quality of the leather," Lenke said as we stopped and peered through a window filled with footwear of all sorts, "it all looks cheap. We want top quality, not this sort."

"I agree, and we can supply you with the very best." I nodded.

Sure enough, most of the things we saw were little more than souvenirs; the kinky equivalent of 'kiss me quick' hats! Tourists pour in to Amsterdam's Red Light District and know they have to take something home with them. These are the cheap and cheerful products that they buy.

"When people see Kim wearing your goods, everybody will want to copy her and buy from us." Lenke obviously had it all planned in her head and she was determined that I should understand where she was coming from.

We carried on with our tour, all of us were making mental notes about what we wanted to produce for Kim.

We strolled along the Oudezijds Achterburgwal and Willem and Lenke, in their infuriatingly perfect English, explained where we were going next.

"The Casa Rosso is one of the oldest erotic theatres in the Netherlands and is certainly one of the most famous attractions in our Red Light District. I think you'll like it." Lenke said.

We stopped outside the most amazing building. Tucked in between sex shops and cafés was the brightly lit theatre with a huge pink neon elephant in lights above the canopy and two fountains either side of the main entrance. One was surmounted by another pink elephant and the other was a huge pink phallus. Both were squirting water!

In fact the Casa Rosso has changed quite a lot since I was there; it's now billed as a Theatre and Casino. It still has the neon pink elephant, but the fountains have dried up and since disappeared.

"Here we are. The Casa Rosso." They both beamed.

It really was an eye-opener. It was the first, and certainly the last, time I'd ever been to a place like this. It was weird. I'd psyched myself up. I didn't want them to think I was the little boy from the back streets of puritanical England. I was torn. I didn't want to go in but at the same time I did!

My conscience was playing Devil's advocate. I'd got the Devil on one shoulder urging me on and an angel on the other shoulder trying to hold me back. They were fighting. Yet again, was this a step a Boss should take? I was suffering. The Devil was winning. "It was work," I told myself. The angel had lost the fight! I could see her clasping her hands over her eyes; she'd given me up as a lost cause!

But that step over the threshold was a big, hard step to take. A leap of faith. Once in the auditorium we found seats at the back. We were faced with an empty, dimly lit stage. The house lights went down and the stage lights came up. A man and a woman walked on, dressed as a doctor and a nurse.

They went through the crazy pretence of 'setting up' a story (quite why, I never knew) with a script I couldn't understand but knew exactly where it was going to lead. The clothes came off quickly and then they performed a rather gymnastic, aerobic and intense routine with all the passion of a couple choosing wallpaper at a local DIY store!

They staggered to their feet, turned to their audience and, like all 'Am Dram' performers, waited for the rapturous applause. As it turned out, it was a rather pathetic, slow hand-claps that sounded like someone had brought a seal in from the cold, tempting it with a wet fish!

They walked off. That was it! I thought, "That wasn't very erotic."

It wasn't what I expected; I wasn't embarrassed by it, but I certainly wasn't excited by it. It was just so bizarre. I was confused. I'd expected something more like the Folies Bergère: alluring, sexy, tempting, subtle and highly erotic. But this! It was as thrilling as a third-rate Benny Hill sketch without the fun and certainly without the sauciness of a 'Carry On' film.

Unfortunately, Willem and Lenke sensed my lack of interest and they could see I wasn't really thrilled by it. Probably it had something to do with the way I was peering into my now empty beer glass!

"So what do you think?" Willem looked me in the eye.
"To what?" I asked. Did he mean the beer? The décor? Or what?
"The theatre, the stage, the whole setting. This is where we're going to do the photo shoot tomorrow." He sounded more excited, "Because tomorrow, it'll be your turn on that stage!" I gulped.

We had a quick refill and a few words about the plans for the next day. We left early and found the car. We went to the hotel leaving me to come to terms with all that had happened in this extraordinary day.

The following morning the thought of last night's experience was still surging through my brain. What would today bring I wondered?

I'd still not met the lovely Kim in the flesh. Back we went to the Casa Rosso with the two suitcases. Kim was to meet us outside. We waited and waited. By now I was thinking it would never happen and then, all of a sudden, as if from nowhere, came this cloud of perfumed fluff!

"Steve I'm SO sorry. Willem, Lenke darling, oh forgive me for being SO late." She bubbled and then she turned to me. "I saw the programme, Steve, wonderful. All your fantastic clothes and the boots, how I lo-o-o-ve the boots!"

It was like being hit by a giant marshmallow. She was amazing, I couldn't help warming to her; she was one of the nicest people imaginable; she put me at my ease from the first moment.

We went into the empty theatre and on to the stage. Thank goodness we were just a small group, Willem, Lenke, Kim's husband and a stage manager who put the lights on for us!

Kim quickly shed her feathers and furs and dived into the cases full of the samples I'd brought. Kim's husband took some fantastic shots of her and directed her in all manner of poses. She changed into outfit after outfit; leather for a few shots, then into some metallic wear for a few more.

Then Kim's husband called, "Steve, your turn."

I froze for a moment.

"I've only got some black leather trousers and boots."
"That's fine," he said, "We want you to join Willem and pose with Kim between you. Two men in black and her, super! Kim posing with her masters!"

I felt like a wimp! Rugby player I may be, but Willem was a typically tall Dutch man with a Van Dyke moustache and goatie under his bottom lip; I believe it's called a 'soul patch'. He looked like D'Artagnan, a manicured Musketeer.

Anyway, everyone was happy with the result. Kim was over the moon while Willem and Lenke kept us all supplied with friendly banter and a bottle of wine. Truth to tell, I was glad it was all over!

After the shoot we all went for lunch. It was one of those occasions when you have to pinch yourself because you can't quite believe it's happening! There I was sitting in a restaurant in Amsterdam with some valuable new customers, watching Holland's top porno star eating the biggest plate of sausage and fries I've ever seen.

It amused me then, and it still makes me laugh now when I think of it. Kim stabbing the sausage with a fork and teasing her lips with it before taking a bite! It was rather more erotic than watching the Doctor and Nurse's un-erotic sketch of the night before!

We talked and talked over the meal. It was now that I couldn't resist asking Kim all those questions I'd been dying to ask her. How did she feel doing all of her stage shows, photographs and films in front of her husband who was also her cameraman and photographer? How did it affect their relationship? I was being so nosey, but I needed to know the answers.

"Oh no, that's work," Kim laughed dismissively, "what we do at home is our business; what goes on in the studio is something else altogether."

She was so matter of fact. I couldn't grasp it. She wasn't in the least bit offended that I'd asked and it obviously worked for them.

We then went on to discuss the photo shoot and the future. Willem invited me back to Amsterdam with my team for a Dutch Erotica Show. That, again, was an offer too good to turn down.

Quite unexpectedly, my time in Holland had been far more rewarding than I could have imagined. It resulted in customers I knew could be trusted, plus a huge order and the prospect of another trade show. I couldn't wait to share the news back in Earls Barton.

Three weeks after I arrived home a package arrived in the post. It was from Holland and I presumed it would be a pile of photographs from the shoot. It turned out to be a selection of Dutch porno magazines. I really didn't know what to do with them.

Thank goodness they'd been addressed to me personally otherwise the parcel might have been opened by one of my unsuspecting staff! But in a way, I do half wish I could have been a fly on the wall watching Rosie or Clarice opening the package!!! I'd love to have seen their faces. What a picture that would have made!

I had the speediest flick through one or two and then I happened to see the word 'Divine'. I turned back to the double page centre spread and there, in glorious Technicolor, was a picture of ME with Kim.

The list of my 'claims to fame', dubious or otherwise, was getting longer by the week! Now I was a centre-fold pin up in a Dutch porno magazine. What next?

"Kinky Boots have no boundaries, only in your imagination."
Steve Pateman

XVII

Sun, Sea, and Sexy Scarborough!

A few weeks of normality followed when we could fulfil orders, both in our usual output and also in the 'Divine' range. Then one morning I had a phone call from Martine, the Editor of a journal called 'Rose's Repartee'. It describes itself as a 'transgender and cross-dressing life-style magazine'.

It's not in the least salacious. Indeed, it really is a serious life-style magazine with intelligent and well-written articles. There's lots of advice and, of course, fashion!

The reason for the call was that Rose's Repartee wanted to do a feature on 'Divine' along with an advertisement for our goods. It sounded perfect. Here was an opportunity to aim our products directly at the people who really wanted them.

We had an advert designed and a journalist came and met me and looked at the factory. In due course, a double-page article appeared in the magazine. I was extremely impressed and it did us nothing but good, with orders pouring in.

A month later Martine rang again. She had an even better offer!

"Steve, I didn't tell you when we spoke before, but I wonder if you'd be interested in a very special event in Scarborough that we organise and would be 'right up your street'!" She sounded enthusiastic.
"OK," I said, "tell me more."

"Well," she went on, "each November we take over an entire hotel for what we call our 'Harmony Weekend'. We've been holding them since 1988 and they're a huge success. The hotel's got a big room, like a ballroom, and we invite companies to come and exhibit their products."

"What sort of companies?"
"All sorts," came the reply, "suppliers of make-up, wigs and hair products, breast enhancement, clothes, lingerie and hopefully your boots and shoes."

It sounded like a brilliant idea. It was almost like a mini 'Erotica' with a hotel filled with a captive audience all eager to buy!!

The only cost, she said, was for our bed and board; there'd be no charge for a stand in the exhibition hall. Even better! So Stan and I started to plan a stand and a stock list of what we'd take.

On a chilly Friday morning in November, Stan and I drove our tightly packed Transit Van up to the hotel on the Yorkshire Coast wondering what we'd find and what would happen over the next day or two.

We arrived just before lunch and were well received by the helpful staff. It took us some time to set the stand up in the big room and to make sure the stock was logically stored for easy access in case we were hit with an invasion of over-eager shoppers!

Once we were sorted, we went into Reception to ask if we could get some sandwiches and a beer before everybody arrived. What hadn't occurred to us before was that the vast majority of the guests were going to be men. There were some accompanied by their girlfriends or wives, but all of them had one thing in common. From the moment they checked in and went to their rooms, they took on their female persona. 'He' may arrive as 'John', but after check in, 'she' then becomes 'Jane'.

All our previous conceptions, possible inhibitions or hang-ups flew out of the window. Here was a closed community, escaping the cares of the outside world and simply being themselves. We were soon to learn what a wonderful group of people they were. No one seemed to have a problem! If we had shown any discomfort, the issue was ours and ours alone. Everyone else was relaxed and, most of all, they were all determined to have a great time.

What was most wonderful to me was that the men who came with their wives, girlfriends or partners, had their full support. It was incredibly warming to see how the women were completely at ease with their beautifully dressed partners.

What's more, they enjoyed a bit of banter with us. They were all ready and willing to open up to us and to talk about themselves. They wanted to tell us what they were 'in to', what they desired most and what they wanted from us. We almost felt like confidantes, therapists and yes, their friends. It was incredibly humbling.

The exhibition started in the early afternoon. We opened the stand and trading began. The interest was incredible and so were the guests. Of course there was a huge amount of banter. The jokes and double-entendres caused screams of jollity. There was no nastiness, no bitchiness. They were, in their words, "all girls together" having a ball.

One really lovely 'girl' came in fully dressed, I don't know what her real name was but she introduced herself as 'Madge'. She must have been well into her seventies, even a touch older, and she was dressed to suit her age. 'Twin-set and pearls' is the best description. The trouble was she couldn't bend down to fit on the knee-length lace-up boots she'd chosen. It was up to Stan and me to get down on all-fours and help her. We took a leg each!

So there we were on the floor with 'Madge' sitting on a stool, legs akimbo, her skirt pulled up to give us easy access to her legs, with us trying to get her feet into the boots.

Suddenly Stan nudged me and indicated upwards. We both looked up and there, under the skirt we saw the un-feminine parts of 'Madge' tumbling out of the silky lace French knickers, all at eye-level! It was all we could do to keep straight faces because naturally, the last thing we wanted to do was offend 'Madge'. We eventually got her into the boots and she was thrilled.

We realised it was getting near to dinner time, so we closed up the stand and went up to our room for a quick tidy up. That done, we went downstairs. There was a series of landings and stairs winding down to the hall and as we drew nearer to ground level, the air was heavy with something that we couldn't quite identify.

But once on the final landing, we realised what it was. It was as if someone had let a prize bull loose in Boots' perfume department and it had smashed every bottle. The over-whelming mixture of aromas seemed to engulf us. We could hardly breathe. It was unbelievable. You almost needed a sharp knife to cut through it!

The hall, bar and lounges were packed with the most beautifully dressed people looking absolutely amazing amidst this haze of a powerful, intoxicating perfume sweeping over us. As we landed in the hall, everyone turned to look at us. It suddenly dawned on us why. We were the only two blokes dressed as men!

There were ball gowns, slinky numbers, little black dresses; every sort of outfit imaginable. It was like a fashion parade with us as the token men!

We made our way to our table. We were sharing it with six others, Stan and I felt like fish out of water because we were the only two blokes surrounded by all this glitz and glamour.

After a while, we overcame our embarrassment at seeing men in wigs, dresses and full make-up, and we started talking.

Within ten minutes the girlie chat subsided and we forgot these were men dressed as women, and we were talking about 'bloke' things, rugby, football, fishing and golf; the sort of things men talk about when they're gathered round a table.

Every so often Stan and I had a kind of reality check. We had to remind ourselves that we were talking about manly hobbies and interests with men dressed in all this finery. What impressed us, and made things easier for us, was that they shared the funny side of the situation. They laughed at our embarrassment and what's more, they were quite happy to laugh at themselves. They were so nice and treated us so well.

All the members of staff were brilliant with us too. In a way we were the ones who were the odd ones out and for that reason, they were all concerned that we were OK.

"You're not dressing tonight?" One of the waiters whispered to Stan as he put down a bowl of soup.
"No, we're here with the trade stands." he said assertively!
"Sorry," the waiter went on, "anyway, just to let you know, the female staff have to use the Gent's loos because all the Gents are in the Ladies doing their hair and make-up."
"Er, thanks, for letting us know." Stan and I chorused.

Bright and early the next morning we had breakfast and went straight to the ballroom to open our stand. We were really busy with customers. They took ages to choose and buy because they chatted so much to us. They all knew about the Kinky Boot Factory programme and wanted to find out every detail of the show. By the afternoon, we were reeling the Kinky Boot story 'off pat'!

Just after lunch a man in jeans and an open-necked shirt came to the stand and hovered for a while. He said he'd arrived late but was anxious to look at some shoes as he needed a special pair for one of his outfits.

He was an ordinary guy but what caught my eye was his absolutely stunning girlfriend. They talked for ages about the BBC 2 TV programme and even treated us to a couple of beers. They were really great characters and kept us entertained for a good half an hour. They bought some shoes and off they went. We arranged to meet them later in the bar.

Then came the evening's events. After the Gala Dinner it was Show Night. It was a big party and everyone came down looking even more glamorous than they had the night before. It was all 'teeth and tiaras'!

The highlight of the evening was the 'Miss Repartee' beauty contest. It's the same as any other beauty contest, ten contestants parade around holding numbered cards. The compere questioned them all in turn and, just like Miss World, they all said they loved animals and wanted world peace!!

There was cheering and wolf-whistles and the audience had as much fun as the contestants. The winners were chosen and announced in reverse order and when the winner's name was read out, the place went wild! She was given the obligatory sash and was crowned with a sparkling tiara and, of course, she cried!

Then came the raffle and we'd both bought tickets and, as luck would have it, Stan won one of the prizes. Now Stan is one of those guys who, even after a close shave, still has a dark beard line. Guess what, Stan's prize was a three-part laser hair removal and facial treatment in a beauty salon! Thank goodness he has a good sense of humour! It was now my turn to laugh.

The next event of the evening was the disco. We decided this was the time to head for the bar because the disco was bound to be a flop. After all, it's a well-known fact that blokes don't dance at discos. So naturally, all these gloriously dressed girls would sit this one out. Wrong!

No sooner had the compere said the disco would go on until midnight, than there was a stampede as all the 'girls' with handbags swinging made for the glitter-ball-sparkling centre of the dance floor. It was like a rugby scrum. All the handbags were thrown into the middle and the dancing began.

But it wasn't like women dancing; it really was 'dad-dancing', the old-fashioned twist movements that men have perpetuated as an excuse for dancing for the past fifty years!

I followed Stan to the bar, happy to escape. We leaned on the counter and chatted away about the incredible evening that was unfolding around us. Then, suddenly I felt a tap on my shoulder. It was a gorgeous girl.

"Hi-ya Steve, how are you doing? Enjoying yourself?" I had no idea who she was but I was pretty flattered that this lovely creature had chosen to come and chat to me.

"Wow," I said, looking her up and down, "You look fantastic."
"Do you like it? Oh, I'm so glad," she went on, "I'm wearing the shoes, what d'you think?" She indicated to her feet beautifully encased in a pair of our 'Divine' diamanté stilettos."

Out of the corner of my eye I could sense Stan fidgeting. He obviously wanted to tell me something. In the end I looked his way and he whispered, "You've no idea have you? She's the guy with the gorgeous girlfriend who bought us drinks earlier in the Show Hall."

I did what I always do at times like this; I blushed scarlet and looked her up and down.

"Oh Yes," I said unconvincingly, "you look fabulous." Her equally gorgeous girlfriend was killing herself laughing because she clearly realised that I hadn't got a clue who her stunning partner was.
"You fancy her, don't you?" she chuckled saucily. They both reeled with laughter and the 'girl' said in her normal voice, "I got you there, didn't I?"

"You certainly did. I really didn't recognise you." I had to admit it.
"Not even the shoes?" She did a mock ballet pose and pointed her toe and proudly waggled her new shoe. "I think they're fab. I've simply got to buy more tomorrow. But for now, we're going to hit the dance floor!" And off they went.

We ordered another drink and stood at the bar people watching! Over on the far side of the room there were three beautifully dressed 'girls', all very much worse for wear judging by the stack of empties on the table. They were having a lively debate.

"What's going on over there?" I whispered to the bar man.
"Don't worry," he smiled as he looked over to them and carried on drying a glass, "they come every year and it's always the same."
"Don't the other guests object? Stan asked.

"Good grief no," the young chap replied, "they're part of the fun. They were all in the forces during the Falklands War. The one in green was in the army, that one in the red top was in the Royal Navy and the other one always wears blue, she was in the Royal Air Force. They just love to relive it all and argue as to who was most effective at Goose Green or whatever! They're quite harmless and besides, they're good for the bar trade!"

Then we noticed another 'girl' propping up the bar just a little away from us. She looked lonely, so now the more 'liberated' Stan, said, "You all right?"
"Aye, I'm fine." She murmured in a strong Glaswegian accent, "fine."
"Are you enjoying yourself?" Stan went on.
"Aye, aye, sure. I'm fine." She had obviously been drinking quite a lot over the evening and her speech was beginning to slur a little.

It was getting late and her outfit was showing the signs of the time of the evening; her wig was askew, her eye shadow and make-up were smeared, her sapphire blue, very clinging, dress that earlier must have looked stunning, was riding up, her stockings and suspenders were riding down. She looked as though she was on a bit of a boozy session.

The funniest thing about her was that, as she leaned on the bar, she didn't have a nice little glass of gin and tonic as you might expect, but she had a big bottle of Newcastle Brown Ale with a straw in it and from time to time she'd put the straw to her lips to take a sip.

It looked so incongruous. Anyway, to cheer her up I said, "You look absolutely amazing."
"Och, thank you, that's very nice of you," her face lit up as she spoke, "we like to make an effort you know."
"And it shows," I said, "would you mind if I asked you about the Harmony Weekend?"

"No problem," she said and slid her bottle a little nearer to us, "what d'you want to know?" She moved closer to us with her elbows still on the counter.

Actually, I wanted to know a lot, but I didn't want to intrude too far and I certainly didn't want to upset her. What I really wanted to ask, but daren't, was why did she drink Newcastle Brown Ale from a bottle with a straw? I resisted the urge!

She was so open and willing to talk. Once Stan and I had asked her a few general questions she suddenly started to tell us all about herself. She blurted out, "And I bet you can't guess what my hobby was?" She put her bottle down on the counter and stood to her full height as she posed the question. She was very heavily built.

"Er, gardening? Sport? Rugby?" I volunteered.
"You'd never guess," she laughed out loud, "I was a power-lifter."
A huge grin came across her face.
"Really?" Stan was moderately disbelieving as he surveyed the outfit and the shoes.

"Aye, those were the days. I know it's hard to believe with me dressed like this, but you can't always judge a book by its cover."
"Well," I said, "you still look fit and well and you look great dressed up tonight."
"Och, you're too kind," she put her hand on Stan's shoulder, "too kind to an oldie!"

"But can I ask just one more question?" I couldn't resist this last intrusion. I just had to know.

"Go on." She said.
"Why the bottle and straw?" I said, "Why don't you have a glass of gin and tonic, Bacardi and Coke, something like that, more fitting to your wonderful appearance?"
She looked me straight in the eye and tossed her head back.

She roared with laughter and in her thick Glaswegian accent said, "I don't wanna ruin my lippy, now do I?"

With this Stan and I burst out laughing. Our new-found friend suddenly joined in and she suddenly realised what she'd just said. "Aye I canna be doing' wi' those posh drinks, I'd rather stick to me beer!!"

After a fun-filled, incredulous, unreal night, a night of such fun and new experiences, Stan and I retired to the sanctuary of our own room. The next morning we had a half-day of selling before we had to break the stand down and make our way back to Earls Barton.

The show at Scarborough, the hotel, our new customers and new-found friends, even to this day, hold a very special place in my memories and it's one of the best 'blokes' weekends I have ever been on.

"Heels are good for the sole!"
Steve Pateman

XVIII

The Big Screen

Yet another phone call! Nowadays all these business dealings would be by email, but in those (not-so-far-off) days all communication was by phone, fax or by letter. But there was a disadvantage…

The phone rang almost continuously after the success of 'Trouble at the Top' and many of the calls came to nothing. Television companies, magazines, all sorts of media organisations showed an interest and dipped their toes in the Kinky Boots pool, but only a few took the plunge and followed it up.

So when, one December day, Rosie buzzed me while I was down on the factory floor to say that there was a call from a film company, my heart sank.

Now, don't get me wrong; the idea of a film company contacting me would normally have filled me with excitement. But in December, the last thing I needed was distraction from the main task. In any shoe factory, the months leading up to Christmas are always the busiest. There simply aren't enough hours in the day to get all of our production done.

We had the added stress of completing all the new orders and samples from Düsseldorf, as well as all our new mail order demands from Erotica, to say nothing of the huge response from Scarborough!

On this particular December day it seemed that anything that could go wrong was going wrong. I was getting pretty frayed round the edges! We'd had machine break-downs; supplies hadn't come in, deadlines were creeping up on us far too quickly; staff were off sick; it was one of those days that really was going pear-shaped.

Add to all this the fact that, as I hinted just now, most of these media calls don't come to fruition, I really wasn't up for taking the call.

But I went to the nearest phone. Boy, do I regret what happened next!

"Yes? Steve Pateman. How can I help?" I must have sounded really bolshie. "Hello, my name is Peter, I'm with Harbour Pictures in London. I've been told all about you and the BBC 'Trouble at the Top' programme. It's such a good story. I believe it has the potential to make a great film. I mentioned it to Nick Barton, who runs Harbour Pictures and he said he'd seen the TV programme as well, and totally agrees with me; it's a film that just has to be made."

As he went on, all I could see were the piles of shoes and boots not being processed and put on the racks. Sadly I was rather short with him.

"I'm sorry, I really don't have time for this. Our customers are my priority," I took a breath, "if you're still interested after Christmas and you think we're good enough, contact me in the New Year." With that I ended the phone call and went back to what I was doing.

Christmas came and went. All the orders went out, the customers were all supplied, we all had our break and soon after New Year the factory was back to full running order.

January is the time for doing all the things that were not urgent enough to be done last year. I had a pile of letters to be answered and other office work to attend to. I just happened to put my hand in my smock and I felt a piece of paper. On it was Peter's name and number.

Then that flash of guilt hit me. I'd been so off-hand and dismissive on the phone to him. I wouldn't blame him if he decided not to come back to me because of my unforgivable manner.

So I rang him.

"You're not going to shout at me, are you?" Peter didn't mince his words but I think he was joking.
"No, I'm really sorry about my response back in December, I'm afraid you caught me on a really bad day." I hope I sounded genuine.
"Don't worry, we all get them." He sounded calm, polite and very understanding.

"Anyway, let bygones be bygones and start afresh. How can I help? You see, we get a lot of interest from all sorts of people and so often nothing comes of their enquiries, I've wasted so much time and effort and my hopes have been dashed numerous times when it all falls through. So I do get a bit suspicious."

"Careful Steve", I thought, "New Year's resolution, new beginnings, new ideas, new projects? Who knows?"

"Well, I can imagine how you feel, but we're more serious than most." He paused for a moment, "Have you heard of the Calendar Girls? They're the Women's Institute members up in Yorkshire, they posed for a calendar for charity with…"
"Yes, I know what you mean," I butted in, "they all stripped off for it."

The calendar had been the talk of one of our Round Table meetings as we we'd considered doing a male version for charity.

"Well," he continued, "we've got the rights to make their story into a feature film and we're actually in the early stages of pre-production as we speak."
"OK?" All of a sudden, he'd won my full attention.
"And your story would fit in very well with our future plans. It's a very British story with ordinary people doing extraordinary things. It would be a winner." He was silent, waiting for a reaction from me.

He didn't have to wait long. "Wow!" I said. "Er, yes, I'm certainly interested. Where do we go from here?"
"For a start," said Peter, "I'd like to come and see you, have a meeting, talk about everything, toss a few ideas around and take it from there."
"That would be great." So we set a date for him to come. It was the perfect time of year for planning new projects.

He came. He looked round the factory, met some of the staff and workforce. I showed him photos from the TV show and also our catalogues. He was with me for most of the day. We went to the pub for lunch and that gave him a chance to see a bit of the village.

He was such a nice guy. We'd immediately clicked and I really grew towards him. After all, he'd made the effort to come up to see me rather than get me to go to him. That was promising and all he said made me certain that he was genuinely interested in our story.

"I'm really excited about this," he said over coffee back at the factory, "I need to go back to share all this with my partners at Harbour Pictures. I'll keep in touch and let you know."

I promised to keep all this under my hat for the time being even though I was dying to tell everyone. Anyway, two weeks later he phoned again.

"Steve, we've all done a lot of talking this end. We managed to get a tape of 'Trouble at the Top'. We really think this could make a terrific film."

"That's great." I responded enthusiastically.

He went on, "I'm planning to come up with Nick Barton and Suzanne Mackie, also producers at Harbour Pictures. We'd like to meet you and look round the surrounding area; I want to visit some of the old factories in the county. I want to get a feel of what the shoe trade was and how it is now. I want to meet people, talk to them, visit the Shoe Museum and immerse myself in boots and shoes!"

His excitement was infectious. I couldn't wait to meet him again. I was keen to share the magic of shoemaking with him, as well as with Suzanne and Nick.

I showed them round the factory. When they first saw a pair of thigh length boots in red patent leather being cut, their eyes lit up. This was, for them, the moment of belief in the story. This was the defining moment. They were so struck by the powerful image of red patent boots being made. Nick said, "We've just got to have a pair for 'show and tell'! We need to have them in the office to inspire us and those around us."

With that they purchased a pair of sexy, red patent, thigh length Kinky Boots. It was at this point that I began to believe in them. They had that look in their eyes; the same look that I had when I first came into contact with Kinky Boots. Yet again those powerful boots had worked their magic.

As I was so busy I called on my Dad to help show them round the County. He took them to some of the old shoe-making villages where once the factories were the main place of employment, but now were ghostly reminders of their former past. He also told them loads of stories, anecdotes of the trade and all about the characters who worked and lived in the area.

They went round Northampton's Boot and Shoe Quarter where once there was a shoe factory on virtually every corner and where now most of them have been converted into trendy apartments.

Dad took them to the Central Museum in Northampton where the National Shoe Collection is housed and Peter quizzed the experts about the history and economy of Northamptonshire's shoe trade. They were obviously interested in every aspect of shoemaking; the research was invaluable to them because they were keen to make the film as authentic as possible.

They went back to London to make plans and to discuss the future of their 'New Project'. The next step was for me to go to London for a meeting with the Harbour Pictures partners and team. We met and I simply told my story. Every detail. They asked loads of questions and took reams of notes. I was surprised at how excited they were about my story. They all agreed that it had the potential to make a fantastic film. But then they dropped a bit of a bombshell.

"You do realise that nine out of ten British films never hit the big screen," said Nick. His words really brought me back down to earth. "It's all very well having the idea and the story, but without the financial backing, the majority of movies die before they are born."

"So what are the chances of my story making it then?" I looked round the table as I spoke. "Is this one of the nine, or could it be the one in ten?"

Peter, ever the optimist, piped up, "As far as I'm concerned it's the 'one in ten'. We've managed to get backing for Calendar Girls, which is another very British story; they loved that so they'll love this, it would be an ideal 'follow-on'. That's definitely going to count in our favour with the big boys. But first things first, we have to get a working script and that's what sells it to them. So having you as an insider, an expert, to help us will be invaluable."

This was good news for me. To be involved from the start was important because I was a little wary of how the British film- makers would handle the story. Would they give it too much of a Hollywood slant? The BBC had been brilliant. They'd shown us in a really good light and had been true to the story.

Would a big screen movie do the same? How much would they change of what really happened? How would they show the industry, our factory, our workers, our customers, our friends and family? It was yet another act of faith. After all, it was my story; it was my idea, our lives and our future. Once again I felt that cold chill creep across me. Was this to be another step too far?

If you count the worldwide viewing, up to ten million people knew about my Kinky Boots and 'The Kinky Boot Factory' from the 'Trouble at the Top' series and they knew the way it was told. It was a documentary and it was factual and truthful. It had been a great success, so how do you improve on that without distorting the truth or over glamorising it?

I was at a loss! How on earth could they make it work as a film? The Kinky Boots might be the 'stars', but it was the people who wore them and brought them to life. They were my main concern. I had always been protective of my story. But now I'd grown to be even more protective of the real people who had allowed us into their world. The men, the women and the 'girls' who had bought the boots and shoes and had given us a new lease of life.

We had always treated our customers with the utmost respect and we'd gained their trust. The last thing I wanted to do was to see them ridiculed or shown in a bad light. I'm always up for a bit of 'glam' but not at the expense of the many truly wonderful customers and new friends that we'd come to know and love. Would they use too much artistic licence and trivialise something we now take so seriously?

Following on from the commissioning of Calendar Girls with Harbour Pictures, Nick, Suzanne and Peter had many meetings with Buena Vista International, part of the Disney Corporation, who expressed the same interest. They were so keen that they commissioned the first stage of getting a working script put together.

The first scriptwriter was found, and a meeting was arranged. I told her my story; she recorded it as well as asking loads of questions and scribbling pages and pages of notes. We discussed the television programme, the shows, Düsseldorf and Erotica, the stories, the anecdotes, learning to walk in boots, shaving my legs, the wonderful people and characters that we'd met on our fabulous journey.

The first script arrived on my doormat. It wasn't what we'd hoped for. The writer had totally missed the point. She was a Northerner and she'd made Earls Barton and our factory sound like Blake's Jerusalem; dark, gloomy, 'Satanic Mills' with 'Eee bah gum' and 'Ecky thump' type characters! No way was this any longer a story about Northamptonshire.

So it was 'goodbye' to that script and its writer. After this, Geoff Deane was brought in to write the script. He did a remarkable job and the story started to come to life. Geoff did quite a few drafts and each one got better.

However Nick, Suzanne and Peter believed it still needed something extra and at this stage they brought in another great writer, Tim Firth. With his recent success with them on 'Calendar Girls' he was definitely the right man for the job. With his input the story was nearly there.

At last we had writers who really understood what it was all about! They brought out the light-hearted humour and the emotions and, what was the most wonderful surprise to me; it had become a story with a message. It was magnificent. They made the whole thing leap off the page.

Many might imagine that when a big film company takes your story and adapts it for the screen you, the subject, will be paid millions. Nothing is further from the truth!

A payment was received from Harbour Pictures to hold the option on the story to ensure that I didn't sell it to anyone else. From then on there would be 'stage payments' at intervals as the project progressed.

Anyway, with a working script ready to go, the next step was that the backers wanted to meet me. 'Oh hell,' I thought, 'is it all going to rest on me?' Now they wanted to hear the story and the passion straight from the horse's mouth.

So off I went once again to London with my trusty squeaky suitcase and a stomach once more filled with butterflies.

It was a nerve-racking experience; walking through the big doors of the Disney Building, This was the 'big time'. I was on hallowed ground. The vast entrance hall was lined with what looked like one-armed bandits in an amusement arcade. In fact they were accounting machines, each with the name of one of their new blockbuster films above it and on each, a screen showed the amount of money that film was grossing, minute by minute worldwide.

We were to meet in a boardroom upstairs. It was as big as a tennis court, plush and sumptuous. The walls were adorned with stills from Disney films and all round the room were massive porcelain figures of Disney characters: Snow White, Pinocchio and Bambi. They were all there. Some of them actually on the table in front of me.

We made our polite introductions and they asked if I had any of the Kinky Boot range with me. From my suitcase I pulled a few of my samples and carefully placed them on the enormously long table that occupied the entire length of the room. The vivid, red, shiny, PVC Kinky Boots seemed to fill the room with their sensual presence; their aura radiated a forbidden sexiness that seemed so totally out of place in a haven of Disney innocence!

My hosts showed genuine interest. We talked for a good hour and a half and the meeting went really well. It was followed by a lunch in a local restaurant. We'd covered just about everything and anything. It was so congenial that, for the very first time, I felt this really could become a reality.

I left on something of a high. After all, just sitting in the Disney building had to be the highlight of the most unlikely adventure for the lad from Barton! The BBC was one big shock, but this was the British side of Hollywood. All that remained now was for the potential backers to say that tiny, but important word. "Yes!"

A few weeks went by and keeping quiet about the film was killing me. Dad and Sara knew, but that was all. One of the hardest things in the world is having to keep a big secret for a long time.

With a working script in place it was time for Nick, Suzanne and Peter to bring on board a Director, Julian Jarrold. With his input, Nick and Suzanne helped to polish up the script. After this, Julian and Tim Firth met for the first time to produce the shooting script for the film from Geoff Dean's original. With this in hand it was presented to Buena Vista for approval to make the film. Would they give it the green light to become a movie?

Then came a call from Nick from Harbour Pictures. "We've done it, we've got the backing."

"Wow-ee!" I leapt from office chair with excitement.

"Calm down, Steve." Nick said, "This is just the first positive stage, but we've got a long way to go yet. There's a lot of work to be done before we can really say with certainty that it will happen."

I sat down again with a bump! Of course, what he meant was true and obvious, but deep down I still felt positive. So it was back to the daily routine; back to making the regular stock plus the Kinky range and back to the hardest part, keeping quiet about the film for more agonising weeks.

Obviously there were some formalities and contracts that had to be approved from America, from the Disney Corporation. One of the things I insisted on was that the names of my workforce must be changed. It was important that there was no risk that they could be identified and they mustn't be made to look ridiculous. After all, I had to live with them once the film was made and released.

Over the years, people have asked me, "Why wasn't Earls Barton identified as the location of the film instead of Northampton?" My reason was that if the film wasn't received well, I didn't want the reputation of my home village to be tarnished forever.

Northampton is Great Britain's capital of the boot and shoe making industry and has, therefore, a global reputation. To anyone watching in the rest of the country or even across the world, the small village of Earls Barton probably wouldn't mean much.

As Kinky Boots has become a worldwide sensation, our local 'Bartoners' have now become quite jealous that Northampton has claimed all the credit. You can't win!

At this point I asked if I could share it with my family. It was time to revisit 'the Oracle'; my Dad. There was so much to tell him. I said, "Dad, You remember I told you that a film company is interested in making the Kinky Boots story into a proper film."

"Really?" he said unconvincingly.

"Well, it's going to go ahead. They're filming our story."

"Wow, that's great!" he sounded almost enthusiastic! "Am I in it?"

How could I break it to him? Poor Dad didn't make it past page three of the script! I just had to tell him straight.

"Well Dad, although you're fit and well now, in order to give the story a more dramatic thrust, I'm sorry to say that within the first five minutes of the film we'll be seeing you being buried at your funeral in Earls Barton Churchyard!"

"Bloody hell! Nothing like feeling wanted! Couldn't they find someone good enough to play me then?" he said rather hurt. I didn't know whether he was joking or not.

Eventually he got over the shock and, in fact, he'd make quite a lot of mileage out of this part of the film, as we'll see later.

Nick was brilliant. He kept me up to date with regular phone calls charting the film's progress. Then came the big one.

"We've actually reached the moment you've been waiting for, Steve," he was bursting to tell me, "we've started casting the film."

Did they really have to scrape me off the ceiling? Or did it just feel like it?

"That's fantastic news. So it's really a goer? It really is going to happen?"
"Yes, Steve! Kinky Boots, the movie, is going to go into production."

It really was going to happen!!!

"Heels speak for themselves."
Steve Pateman

XIX

The Making of Lola & Charlie

Appropriately enough, Julian Jarrold, the Director of Kinky Boots, the guys from Harbour Pictures and the rest of the casting crew were actually at a film festival in Hollywood. They were looking for someone to play Lola, one of the two leading characters.

Tim and Geoff had come up with the fantastic idea of creating the central character, Lola, a drag artiste and cabaret singer, who visited the factory in search of some sexy boots and ended up being part of the design team. Although that was pure fiction, I approved because it resulted in some hilarious situations as well as some extremely moving moments.

For some reason I'd had the idea that Lola would be a rather predictable white cross-dresser with a blonde wig and pouting lips, so when they told me that the part had gone to Chiwetel Ejiofor, it was a case of, "Who?" As I mentioned earlier, celebrities are not my strong point!

What I hadn't realised was that he was one of Britain's most sought-after young black actors. Even while he was at drama school Steven Spielberg had spotted him and cast him in his Hollywood movie 'Amistad'. Kinky Boots would be his ninth film!

He'd appeared in several plays in London's West End for which he'd won a bunch of awards, including an Olivier for Best Supporting Actor in 'Blue/Orange' a play at Britain's National Theatre.

Imagine my pride when Kinky Boots was released in the UK and worldwide and it earned Chiwetel a nomination for a Golden Globe for Best Actor in a Musical or comedy!

Since Kinky Boots he's won countless more awards including a BAFTA for 'Twelve Years A Slave' and an Oscar Nomination for the same film. So highly is he regarded in Great Britain that Her Majesty the Queen has made him a CBE, Commander of the British Empire. He deserved the part of Lola!

I innocently asked Nick what was it that earned him the part. "Well, apart from the fact that he's a brilliant actor and singer," he said, "he was the only one who came to the audition with a carrier bag containing a wig. He put the wig on and he WAS Lola! It was instant. He had the part."
"And who's playing me? Ewan McGregor? Hugh Laurie?"

I started thinking about all the British actors I'd heard of. After all, I naturally had big ideas about how I should be portrayed.

"Yes, we've cast him already. He was Owen Lars in 'Star Wars: Episode II - Attack of the Clones' and Episode III – Revenge of the Sith', Gawain in 'King Arthur' and he was in 'Warrior' and 'the remake of 'The Great Gatsby'."
"Wow! What's his name?" I was impressed, but who was he?
"He's Joel Edgerton, he's Australian."
"Oh! OK." An Australian playing me? I couldn't quite get my head round it, but I trusted them; I had to! And of course it paid off.

The producers wanted me to help Joel out. They asked me to make a recording of how shoes are made explaining all the terms we use and give him an idea of how I talk in my Northamptonshire accent. So I put the whole story on tape just so that Joel could replace his Australian lilt with my 'Barton' English!

To be perfectly honest, when I saw the film I couldn't detect any Australian accent at all. He did a marvellous job!

If you've seen the film or the musical of Kinky Boots, you'll be aware that the two main characters are Charlie Price, that's the reinvention of me; and Lola, the drag queen.

You may have noticed that here in the true story, there was no Lola. So how did the colourful, outrageous and brilliant Lola come about?

When the scriptwriters were adapting my life for the screen it became clear that the way 'Trouble At The Top' unfolded, the fortunes of W. J. Brookes simply wouldn't be 'dramatic' enough for a major movie.

Dramatic licence had to play its part and there needed to be rather more colourful characters from the outset to engage the audience straight away. Not that our factory isn't interesting, it is, but obviously we were not exciting enough to make the story work!

It would have been too complicated to have several drag queens as leading characters. So Tim and Geoff hit on the idea of making just one, larger than life, outrageous, but totally credible creation. All of my dealings with the real-life, colourful characters and drag artistes that I had met and loved, Tim and Geoff then 'morphed' into one central and unforgettable person.

They called her 'Lola'.

In the film Lola comes to the factory, all dressed in beautiful clothes, big hair, and high heels, the million-dollar look! During her visit she meets Don, an alpha male character in the film who takes a fancy to her.

This is actually a true story, it DID happen. We had a cross-dresser from Luton who turned up, fully dressed in her finery, and she wanted to discuss a joint venture. She was a lovely person; she arrived in a big black Jaguar with her own driver, very posh. She was like royalty!

She insisted on seeing the factory and as we were going round I explained all the different processes. All I could hear were the wolf whistles from some of the men, I apologised for that, but she laughed and said, "Do you think they know who I really am?" Of course, she loved it!

I said, "Don't worry, we can sort that out later!"

So we had our meeting up in the office, which went well with some great ideas. After she left I went back down into the factory to the lasting room.

Remember Bert, the character from the lasting room in the factory? Well, I've always had quite a bit of banter with him and I decided this was the moment for me to score a few points; this was to be my time. Revenge!

All the men were talking about her. "She loved looking around," I said, "what did you think of her? I reckon she fancied one or two of you." I winked. "The leather aprons, the manly look, the sweaty brow, I think that's what she likes. A bit of rough." I said, trying to tempt Bert into my trap.

He chirped in, "She likes a real man does she? Cor, give her five minutes with me and she'd know what a real man can do."

He went on digging this big hole for himself. He had no idea who or what she really was.

"I could see you fancied her." I said, rubbing it in.
"I'll say," Bert said, "I could show her a thing or two."
I decided this was enough and I had to put him out of his misery!
"Yes, Bert, and I bet she could show you a thing or two as well. So if I could arrange an evening with her for you, do you think you could keep up with her demands?"

"Just try me! I'd show her what I've got". He did the old arm bending bit to show off his prowess."
"Well Bert, I think HE could show you a 'thing' or 'two'!!!"
He looked at me blankly. "What, d'yer mean."

"I mean Bert; well done, she is a he. Congratulations on your taste in women."

Everybody else collapsed. Bert, the alpha male, had just proclaimed to the entire factory, that he was going give her the time of her life and he had no idea. How cruel of me, but it was payback time for all the hassle I'd had from him over the years.

It felt so good!

No one had guessed. It was impossible to tell because she looked absolutely fantastic and so convincing. The style, the walk, the perfume, the voice, she was simply amazing. I knew then that if we could supply more customers like her, we'd be made.

I had told this story to all the scriptwriters on numerous occasions and that's where the seeds of Lola were first sown. The only trouble I had with the 'Charlie and Lola' interaction, is that in the film Charlie didn't understand his market, whereas I had actually done a huge amount of research.

I, as a designer and shoemaker, would never have made boots in Burgundy for the 'erotic' market. I know that burgundy's definitely not sexy. It concerned me in case people seeing the film actually thought I might have done that in reality. No way! I knew red patent, black patent and PVC are sexy. Burgundy? NO, NO, Noooooooooo!

I so agree with Lola's iconic line, "Burgundy. Please God, tell me I have not inspired something Burgundy. RED, RED, RED, Charlie boy. RED is the colour of sex! Burgundy is the colour of hot water bottles! Red is the colour of sex and fear and danger and signs that say 'Do…Not…Enter.'"

So Lola and Charlie were born.

"Heels are like stars, they shine brighter at night."
Steve Pateman

XX

Location, Location, Location.

It was about the time that Harbour Pictures' film Calendar Girls was being released. It was a pleasant surprise and a great honour when I was invited with Sara to the World Premiere in London's Leicester Square. It was a very special occasion; a black tie for me and a long dress for Sara.

As we walked down the red carpet, I turned to Sara and said, "Just think, this could be our film in a couple of years."

"Dream on." She said, her eyes roving the cordoned-off area of the red carpet reserved for the stars.

Then a bloke in a uniform pushed me to one side, "Move along, please, let this lady past."

That put me in my place. Sara and I stood to one side as one of the film's big stars, Celia Imrie, graciously glided past. With my record of star-spotting I grumbled "Who do they think they are, pushing me out of the way?"

As the cameras flashed yet again I said to Sara, "Who's that in the candy-striped frock next to her?" Sara rolled her eyes in utter disbelief and said, "Oh come on Steve for heaven's sake, that's Dame Helen Mirren!"

Sara pulled me away from the stars, as I tried to get in behind them both for a photo opportunity. We took our seats and we loved the film. As the credits rolled up at the end, I turned to Sara, "Just like us, small village, big story. Ordinary people doing something pretty special! It really could be us in a couple of years' time. How scary is that!"

That was our first experience of the red carpet and a world premiere. Our film was still in its infancy. Calendar Girls turned out to be a huge success and made Nick, Suzanne and Peter at Harbour Pictures even more determined that the same should happen to Kinky Boots.

Much of the planning for Kinky Boots, the movie, was in place but they still hadn't decided where to film it. Nick phoned me again.

"Steve, do you know of any shoe factory in the area that we could use for a couple of week's filming?"

"Oh Nick, if you only knew what you were asking." It was an impossible request. It was now October, the busiest time for all shoe factories in Northamptonshire. Christmas was fast approaching, and no way could any factory stop production even for a day, let alone for two weeks.

"Nick, all the factories in Northamptonshire will be rushed off their feet at this time of year. Can't you delay it until January?" I knew, even then we were clutching at straws. "What about using one of the empty factories? Sadly, there are quite a few that have closed down."

It's at this point that my story takes a turn for the worse.

Unfortunately, as you'll read in the next chapter, 'Farewell to Brookes's', filming in the original Kinky Boot factory was no longer an option.

But Nick was determined to sort something. Suddenly his role as Producer fired him up. "Can we come up to see you and perhaps you can take us round to look at some of the other factories. We might get a solution once we see how things are?"

"Of course." I was as keen as he was.

Within a week they were in Earls Barton; the Production team, the scene and set designers, the location managers and with me as Consultant. We went to a few factories in the local area and met Managing Directors, factory managers, machine specialists and, in fact, anyone who might help us to solve the problem.

"It has to be a working factory Steve," Nick insisted, "kitting out a disused factory isn't on the cards; the cost, the delay, everything's against that."

Then, as if a Genie in the 'Kinky Boots pantomime' had appeared from out of the blue, the most extraordinary thing happened.

Tricker's have long been one of the famous names in the Northamptonshire boot and shoe making industry. They worked a lot within the Japanese market.

It just so happened that at that very moment, when Harbour Pictures wanted to start filming, the Japanese economy and currency hit a downturn. Tricker's were now suffering exactly the same situation that had hit us when we had our trouble with the German market.

Tricker's were, therefore, short of work and they were prepared to close down production for two weeks. It was a gift for the film company and for them. Tricker's were paid for the hire of the factory, the employees were paid by Harbour Pictures to be 'extras' in the film, the scenic designers had minimal work to do. It was a win-win situation all round.

So the script was in place, backers were providing the money, the film had been cast and the all-important factory location was arranged.

The cameras could roll!

"When timing and location come together, it's a step in the right direction."
Steve Pateman

XXI

Farewell to Brookes's

"Where one door closes, another opens", so said the ever hopeful Don Quixote, but there was a time for me when it didn't seem very likely.

We'd taken a huge loss in America when a customer there went bust and as a result we had to lay some people off. Then the net seemed to be closing around us even more with the constriction of the British pound against the foreign currencies. It was now starting to hit the customers we sold to in England who were then exporting to their customers abroad.

It wasn't just us as manufacturers being hit, it was having a knock-on effect down the line. So when I said that 90% of our production went abroad, it did; although some of it went through one or more 'middle men' before reaching the final buyer.

The 'middle men' who had ordered our products now didn't want them because they couldn't sell them on either. They had warehouses full of shoes just like we had, and now they were cutting back their orders from us as well.

We then started to get the inevitable phone calls, "Steve, sorry but we've got to tell you, we've gone bust." Over a period of about six months we probably had one customer a month going out of business.

We'd had that massive hit in America and more followed. One guy in the North of England phoned. In his case we had all his shoes made and ready to despatch direct to him. He already owed us over £20,000, plus we'd bought in components from abroad especially for his designs, which were now useless to us. So, it was a triple whammy for us.

Some customers were phoning and telling us bluntly "We've gone bust"; others were more honourable. I remember one case in particular it was about two men who were in a partnership. We'd done loads of business with them; £15, 000 to £20,000 a month. Their custom meant a lot of money and regular production that was hard to replace.

One of them phoned and asked to come and see me. "My partner's done a bunk," he said. I felt sorry for him. "He was on the accounts side and I was looking after the customers and sales. He's done a runner. I can't leave things as they are. I want to come to some arrangement with you so I can pay you all we owe."

He came down to sort things out. He continued to pay and even though we lost some money, he had done the right and honourable thing. He'd paid us back as much as he possibly could. It was like the 'old school' shoe trade of years ago, everything was done on a gentleman's handshake; it was honourable and trustworthy. I felt for him. At least he had tried to honour his commitments; more than some of our other customers.

We'd always made sure we had enough money to stay afloat and we'd paid all our suppliers as we went. This we continued to do, but we also had the wages to pay every week and things were getting tight.

I was watching the accounts every week to make sure we were still solvent; I could see who owed us and what we owed to our suppliers. But with our dwindling cash flow, it got to the stage when I had to face the facts. If we carried on going into debt at the same rate like this we'd soon be in a very sticky position and probably have to go out of business.

I'd always tried to be honest and fair. I knew I couldn't run the business into the ground, take all the money and look after number one. I couldn't leave a wake of creditors owing loads of cash because it would ruin them as well. If I did, I would never be able to sleep at night.

To add to our troubles, I had a phone call from the BBC to say they wanted to come up to film a 'revisit' version of 'Trouble At The Top'.

This was the last thing I needed at this time I thought, but on a positive note, I'd never get this kind of free advertising for 'Divine' anywhere else. Any form of good publicity has to be worthwhile. Not only that, it was another form of completing the history of Brookes, a visual record for generations to come.

I told them I didn't mind them coming to do the revisit, but things had changed since they were last here. We'd now had to cease production and were in the final throes of emptying and selling the factory. This seemed to upset them almost as much as it upset me. They remembered how successful the company was during the first programme, but now the economic climate had finally claimed another victim.

I was happy to be part of it again, but I needed them to concentrate on the positives rather than the negatives, as our mail order side of the business was booming. The last thing I wanted was our customers seeing our brand in a less favourable light. They were more than happy to accommodate my requests.

It was time to have a serious talk with my Father and the rest of the Board of Directors to put them in the picture and tell them that we were going to have to close the factory. They asked if there was anything else we could do, like relocating or cutting the workforce again.

Both suggestions were out of the question, it still wouldn't make the company viable. We'd gone through the accounts and looked at every option; the only answer was to close down the manufacturing, shut the factory, have my 'Divine' products made elsewhere and for us to become a wholesale, mail order retail outlet.

The decision had to be made and quickly. We had to bite the bullet. Again I approached the Footwear Union and between us we sorted out everybody's redundancy monies and date of finish.

You would think that after having already made redundancies the task would be easier a second time around. It wasn't. If anything it was worse. It was an end of an era, another factory lost, another nail in the coffin of British manufacturing.

Having to accept the inevitable brought on self-doubt, depression, worry and failure. Then with our new venture, having to put on a brave face was hard. Having to be an upbeat, enthusiastic and outgoing person to our new customers was pure torture. It was now beginning to take its toll on us all, especially on Sara, Dan and the rest of the family.

We had to fulfil all our remaining orders, pay all our suppliers and sell the rest of our machinery to other footwear manufacturers in the county.

What's more we had to finish off all our uncompleted stock; in other words, all the uppers, soles and components had to be made into finished shoes because they were valueless incomplete. At least as shoes we could sell them on, even at a loss, and that was better than throwing the raw materials away.

While we were going through the painful process of clearing the factory, we had to keep fulfilling the 'Divine' orders because this was going to be my new venture. I found a small family-run company in Leicester who would make the 'Divine' range for me, so Stan and Clarice decided they'd stay on and help me to keep it going.

All the special machinery we'd bought for the Kinky Boots was taken up to Leicester; that included all the rolls of material we used, the heels and zips and all of the other major key components. Manufacturing continued; our 'Divine' footwear range was still in production.

We concentrated on making the warehouse next door workable; it was a Victorian terraced house attached to the factory. In my Dad's time the company bought it, knocked a doorway through the wall between the house and the main building to give us a proper despatch area. This helped with our increased production and gave us more space.

We made a small showroom at the front with a smaller despatch area and offices upstairs. All our stock was moved in to our new 'home'.
Our final stage in the closing process would be to seal up that last connection between our warehouse and the old factory. Once again the building would become independent, just as it had been all those years ago, back in my Grandfather's day and also in part of my Father's day.

Stan and I went round the factory with spanners and hammers removing every bit of machinery, heaving and hauling up and down the three flights of stairs. We had huge 'skips' outside that we filled with rubbish, wood etc. and another with scrap metal and machinery we couldn't sell. Stan and I were fitter than we'd been for years!

The day came when we had to hand over the keys. We'd been lucky enough to find a developer who wanted to convert the factory into apartments. That meant we had to go through a huge amount of legal rigmarole, like applying for planning permission, change of usage and site surveys.

There was one major obstacle that we hadn't counted on. As an industrial building with 115 years of trading, the land had to be tested for contamination by acids, chemicals, solutions or material waste that might be harmful in the future.

Fortunately, things went well and we survived all the formalities. But it was just more added pressure, more headaches, and at a time when we were all so low. It didn't get much tougher than this.

Eventually the factory was empty.

It was a time I'll never forget. I'd been in and out of that building since I was knee high to a grasshopper. It was old and dirty; the high windows had glass so thick with years of dust they looked like net curtains.

The stairs creaked even louder now the building was empty. I knew exactly which ones were the squeakiest and I'd worked out, over the years, how to avoid them, especially last thing at night, when I used to do my security checks and turn off all the lights.

But now the rafters, the walls and the stairs echoed at each step. It was an agonising sound, like the dying breath of a wounded beast.

It was as if Brookes's, now an empty shell, knew that shoemaking was no more. Its time had come; the last pairs of boots and shoes had been completed.

I remember my Grandfather, and later my Father, taking me by the hand and showing me the factory. Their pride, enthusiasm and love of shoemaking that passed from father to son, had been ingrained in them and in turn had been ingrained in me from such an early age.

The noise of the machines in the factory used to frighten me as a small boy. They seemed gigantic to me then, towering over me like nightmare monsters, especially when I saw them working.

But now the cast iron metal, the gears and cogs had all gone, now just a hollow, empty space. All that was left was a stain of oil, an indentation on the floor, like a tombstone of recognition to their past. The loss was beginning to hurt; a void that could now only be filled with memories.

The smell of leather used to be everywhere, and that smell has stayed with me all these years. Even after being out of the trade for so long, the smell instantly takes me back to some of the best times of my life: to the factory, the characters, the history, my friends, the struggles, the successes, the happy times of creativity. It's an old world, the industrial past, lost in time, lost to the archives, lost to the annals of history.

It had been as much my home as my real home, as familiar as my bedroom, as welcoming as our lounge. I could have walked round blindfolded and not bumped into anything I knew where everything had been.

But now it was empty. Still. Silent. Ghostly.

As I opened the door and went in I heard the big key clunk in the lock. In my imagination I could see every machine from the biggest to the smallest. The sound from the old clocking-in machine by the front door still 'ticked and tocked'. It seemed so loud; I'd never heard it before, it was always drowned out by the chatter of the employees and the noise of the factory at work.

I could still picture each one of them, the people I'd known for years who shared the building with me, people who were more than employees, they were the life-blood that flowed through the veins of the building that kept it alive. Now all drained away. All gone.

As I stood there alone there was a hollow echo. My footsteps resounded as I walked around; it seemed like a vast open space, bigger than it had even been before. Was this where all that work had taken place? Where were the machines? Why didn't it smell anymore? Where was the noise? The silence was deafening.

I went up the stairs; I remembered they still creaked, but this time I didn't avoid them, I deliberately stepped on them to hear the sound one more time.

Three storeys of big open space with nothing but an odd picture that we had missed still hanging on the wall, a browning notice pinned to a door, a bit of rag tied round the joint of an old compressed airline pipe.

Finally, as I glanced around, my eyes fell on the empty place where Bert's old machine had once been and there, nailed to an old beam, was another sign I'd missed. "Welcome to Kinky Corner". This was a sign of acceptance from Bert; his tongue-in-cheek humour was a final acknowledgement of his dramatic change. A tear rolled down my cheek. He had changed. The Alpha Male had changed. We all had changed and now it was time for the building to change.

Then a noise rescued me and saved me from my memories.

It was Dad. "What are you thinking?" he said breaking the eerie silence. "All sorts. The end of an era. A bit of Barton's history gone. A huge chunk of our family's life had come to an end." I said, with tears threatening to roll again.

"I know, but it had to happen," Dad said, "God knows how we lasted for so long. I've spent hours wondering what we didn't do, what we could have done." He walked around for a moment, looking at the shell that had spawned his entire life's work.

"I've had sleepless nights and plenty of them, wondering the same," I said, "lying awake, trying to find another stick to beat myself with. It's not just us though; it's the whole industry. How can you fight when the odds are against you? Perhaps I was a fool to think I could save W.J. Brookes."

He came to me and put his hand firmly on my shoulder. "Don't you ever blame yourself Steve, you did everything you could to keep it going." Of course he meant it, but at that moment no words could console me; I had failed.

"Could I have done more?" I wanted reassurance.

"Good grief no. What more could you do? We were all on your side. We all realised it really was the end." I reckon he was near to tears as well.

Good old Dad, it had taken him time and courage to understand my new ideas, but he'd come round in the end and had been so supportive and had even championed the cause.

"Maybe without 'Divine' we'd have closed the factory a couple of years ago," he said, "who knows?" Then from nowhere he added, "I'm so proud of you. What you've managed to achieve was above and beyond; with what you've gone through, no one could have tried harder."

One comfort, if it can be called a comfort, was that we'd managed to find jobs in other local shoe factories for all the workers who wished to stay within the industry. That made me feel a bit better and helped to ease the pain, at least something positive had come out of this.

'Divine' was still in production, so perhaps that was the door that had opened after the big one had closed! Maybe things weren't so bleak after all; maybe there was a future.

Then, I'd almost forgotten, the BBC wanted to come back to do more recording. We had to relive it all over again. This was to be from the Trouble At The Top team, it was The Kinky Boot Factory – Revisited". The complete story with an ending as it really happened.

Having been faced with the threat of closure and having been rescued by the Kinky Boots, they wanted to fill in the gaps from the earlier programme and, amongst other things; this one would include the erotic shows and more about the customers.

What really hurt was that they wanted to film the actual handing over of the keys to the developers. I thought long and hard about it, I didn't think I'd be able to get through it; it had been so emotional for me and for Dad.

But in the end I agreed. So when they came with the camera crew, I got Dad to join me and we walked round the empty factory, just as we had in our private moment, but this time with our bravest faces on, we had to do it to camera. In a way, the accent had moved away from me for a while and it was about Dad's life in the factory and what he had built up and how all this was affecting him.

The time came to film the hand-over. There was the developer with his smart suit and tie and his shining white safety helmet and me standing with the big envelope full of keys.

They weren't just keys to a building, they were keys that unlocked memories, successes and failures. They unlocked sealskin fisherman's boots, boots for Russian soldiers, boots for the British army, steel-capped boots for heavy industry. They unlocked winkle pickers, brothel creepers, and yes, even thigh length red Kinky Boots with four-and-a-half-inch stiletto heels.

These keys were the symbol of what W.J. Brookes had stood for, a part of history. They represented the continuity of four generations, handed down from my Great Grandfather to my Grandfather then on to my Father and then on to me. The thought of me not being able to hand them on to my son Dan was now even more poignant than before. Here I was, about to give these keys to a stranger. What had I done? Dan's birth right gone forever.

The factory had not only been my Father's and my life but it had also played a massive part in my Mum, Margaret's, life as well. She had lived through the turmoil of shoemaking with my Father during his working career. It had also formed a huge part of Sara's life; she had supported me, encouraged me and believed in me. It was a part of all our lives. To Dan it was a place where he'd experienced with me, the same feelings that I'd had as a child when I went with my Father.

That man in the hard hat, what did he know about this building? To him it was just bricks and mortar; to us it was a way of life stretching back a hundred and fifteen years. I hated him; I felt nothing but animosity towards him. I didn't want him to take my family heritage away and replace it with strangers who knew nothing about us, who had no place in our factory.

In that moment, the final handing over ceremony, our hearts felt so heavy; a moment in time I want erased from my memory.

I have never been back. The converted factory is only the other side of the village from where I live now. I have been invited on numerous occasions, but I've never been back. I can't go back. I don't think I could ever go back. The emotions are still so raw.

My final act of respect and my parting gift to the factory was a condition I added to the deeds of transfer, that if I could never cross the threshold of Brookes to make shoes again, then I didn't want anyone else going through that iconic doorway. I insisted the front door was bricked up.

That doorway belonged to the Pateman family, to Brookes's and to all who used it as an entrance to their livelihood. That door is closed. Gone, forever. I can never go through that doorway again and I wouldn't want to. There's nothing there for me now.

In the final section of the BBC's 'The Kinky Boot Factory – Revisited' you can see my Dad getting so emotional, then you see me becoming even more emotional because I could see him getting emotional. His life, my life and the factory, all gone. What had we got to show for it? Another monument to a past industry that would no longer produce shoes. The final closure to an era that could never be brought back.

A brick building with a date stone high up on the wall, 'WJB 1889', A big open space, dirty windows, rickety stairs, as silent as the grave. It was a grave, a grave to boots and shoes, no noise, just stillness.

W.J. Brookes was at peace.

"Saying farewell or goodbye is never the end, it's the starting point of memories."
Steve Pateman

XXII

Lights, Camera, Action!

So, the factory had closed. The BBC's second documentary was made and was broadcast. Now it was time to concentrate once more on Kinky Boots - The Movie. It seemed so strange, filming my story in someone else's factory. The true home of Kinky Boots was taking on a new life...and so was I.

It was a terrific honour to be involved, even in some small way, in the film-making. As a consultant, I went to watch as much as I could. On the first day I took Mum, Dad and Sara along to Tricker's.

It's a Grade II listed factory in St Michael's Road right in the centre of Northampton's Boot and Shoe Conservation Quarter. It's a beautiful building. It has an unusual façade of brown ceramic brickwork with foliate decorations designed in 1924 by R.E. Baretrop. It's one of Northampton's more attractive industrial edifices.

Mr R.E. Tricker was a London boot-maker who came to Northampton in 1902 and the company is still going strong. Tricker's now employs some 70 workers making 700 pairs of shoes a week. They proudly supply the Royal Household and are the only Northamptonshire shoemakers entitled to display the coat of arms of HRH The Prince of Wales.

Royalty of another sort assembled at the factory for 'action' on that first day. By now I'd done some research on the cast and realised most of them were seasoned professionals with enviable pedigrees.

It wasn't long before I was introduced to the cast and we soon became good friends. They were the loveliest bunch of people. Everyone working on the film said this was one of the best and happiest productions they'd ever worked on. Everybody got on. There were no Prima Donnas. They all sat and had meals together. It was a family.

While they were in the vicinity, they wanted to shoot all the Northamptonshire sequences in one go. So the next location was home territory, Earls Barton.

This was the section that came near the opening and featured my on-screen Dad's funeral! It was a great occasion for the village when the entire crew descended and took it over. Nothing like this had ever happened there before.

Many local villagers found themselves roped in as crowd scene extras. It was a cause for great excitement. They even used Toby Hunt the Funeral Director in the village and his hearse and Limousine for 'Dad's' funeral.

Their huge trailers, buses, canteen and technical vehicles were parked in the car park at Barker's Shoes, not far from the church. Barker's warehouse was used for one scene so it was good that a another local company was involved as well.

Permission was given by the Diocese of Peterborough to film in the churchyard and to dig a 'grave' for 'my Father'! They had to dig it on un-consecrated ground away from the main graveyard itself.

From the very start of the project I'd hoped to have members of my family in cameo roles. I asked the producers if my Dad could be one of the mourners at his on-screen funeral, and this was agreed; They were quite keen. It would be a quite a press scoop!

One of my biggest regrets was that my Dad was totally against the idea. "You can forget that," he said firmly, "I'm not tempting fate, whatever you say." So that was that! I think it was a decision he regrets, as what a story that would have been; he could have dined out on that for years!

One amusing thing that happened at the funeral was that the scriptwriters and the Director, Julian Jarrold, thought it would be fun to 'invent' a fictitious long-held Northamptonshire boot and shoemaker's tradition. Since father and son were both shoemakers, wouldn't it be good for the son to drop a shoe onto the coffin in the grave along with some soil?

Of course, no such 'tradition' ever existed and I'm certain that when anyone from Northamptonshire saw this sequence in the film they shouted, 'Never!" But I think, if I decide to be buried when I "shuffle off this mortal coil", to quote Hamlet, I might get Dan to chuck a pair of Kinky Boots in after me!

It never ceases to amaze me how gullible some cinemagoers can be. One of our biggest customers, Martin, was the Senior MD of a famous London store. He and my Dad were very good friends, he used to come up regularly and they would always go for an extended business lunch and have a good long chat.

Martin saw the film. He was very sad at the death of Charlie Price's father and he was so moved by the scene of his funeral in Earls Barton churchyard, which he knew quite well.

He must have been confused. Maybe he thought the film was another documentary from the BBC and that my Father had actually passed away, because one day my Mum phoned, "Steve, when you're passing, pop in for five minutes; there's something I want to show you."

Next time I was in the area I did pop in and to my astonishment, Mum showed me a sympathy card that had been sent to her "and family". It was from Martin and his wife expressing their deep distress at the death of "your amazing husband, our very good friend, Richard."

Yes, he actually believed that my Dad had died!! After all, he'd seen it on the screen. This left Mum having to make a very difficult phone call to put Martin right before he and my Father next spoke.

Often Mum and Dad came over to us for a take-away meal. We always ordered it from our local Chinese restaurant. While we waited, we'd go to the pub opposite. Mum and Sara would put the world to rights, whilst Dad and I would have a crafty pint or two.

It was a very old world style pub with high backed wooden bench seats with curtains on rods, making what the English call 'a snug'! As we sat, beer in hand, waiting for our order, we heard a group of 'old Bartonian' pensioners chewing over the local news helped by a few pints.

All of a sudden one of them, in a loud Barton accent, well oiled by the beer said, "And what about that big funeral last week. They even got ruddy cameras to film it as though he were some hoity-toity celebrity."

"What are you crowing on about Frank?" Another chipped in. "It were for that old bugger Pateman." The first voice responded. At this our ears pricked up. We had heard, along with everyone else in the pub, this old boy starting to get on his soap-box.

"Couldn't goo in the cemet'ry like normal folk. Oh no, he had to goo in the churchyard," he ranted on, "he were an old bastard, he were. A Bugger to work for Oi can tell you."

"I'll have him," Dad said, getting a bit annoyed.

"Oi worked for him an' all," volunteered another old timer. "He weren't that bad. You never got on with him 'cos you was always a-moaning and having arguments with him."

Dad added, "And a lazy bugger at that." At which point, Dad, ever the joker said, "That's it. I'm going to let them have it now." He jumped up, knelt on the bench, leaned forward, pulled the curtains back, stuck his head between them and said, "Evening boys. Seeing I'm a miserable old bugger; fancy a beer from a dead man?"

I was helpless with laughter. Dad eventually sat down again with a smile from ear to ear! "That'll teach them," he said, "I thought old Bert would have a heart attack; if you could have seen their faces, they thought the dead had come back to haunt them."

I'm pleased to say that, as I write, my Dad is still fit and well.

While they were filming behind Earls Barton church, there was one lovely moment. Charlie Price, his father and a boy who played the young Charlie, were all off camera. Standing close by was another 'three-tier' family of shoemakers; mine! My father was there, I was there and so was my son, Dan. This made a terrific picture.

Having sat on the wall with the church as a backdrop, the young Charlie and his father then walk down the mound to 'the lake'. When local people see the finished film they often ask, "Where's the lake?" because there is no lake behind the church in Earls Barton.

Well, there again, you can do anything in a film. Father and son miraculously walk from behind the church in Earls Barton to the lake…in Central London! They used the Serpentine in Hyde Park, seventy-three miles away!

There was a lovely picture taken in central Northampton with my Dad, Mum, Sara, Dan, Stan from the factory and me, all talking together in a crowd scene beside All Saints Church in the town centre. This was our only chance at cameo roles. It's the part where 'Lola' and 'Lauren', (Sarah-Jane Potts) go out for coffee and walk past us! Unfortunately, when locals ask where the café is, again, it's miles away in Covent Garden!

Further afield, the film ends with a sequence in Milan. I thought I'd be in for a free trip to Italy to watch. Sadly, they shot the scene in Canary Wharf, East London, only Chiwetel, Joel and Sarah-Jane went with the camera crew to Milan for one short scene in the Piazza del Duomo.

For us though, the most exciting place they filmed was in the night club where Lola did her act. It was shot in the Too2much Club in Soho and that's where, on 2 January 2005, they held the 'Wrap Party' when the film was complete.

Kinky Boots was given a preview screening for the cast and all involved in making the film, as well as an invited audience, at the Odeon, High Street, Kensington on 3 August 2005. And what did I think of it? We were more than happy with how it turned out.

There were moments, however, that caught me out. For instance, it hadn't occurred to me that, when I saw the part where Charlie Price had to make some of his employees redundant, it would upset me so much. It brought back harrowing memories of how I felt when I had to do that very same thing; the worst moment of my working life. Even now as I think about it, tears come to my eyes.

It was also emotional when Lola and Charlie shared their feelings about their relationship with their fathers. Lola was always in the shadow of her father, who was a boxer, but all Lola wanted was to be herself; a cross-dresser, a top drag artiste with a guilt-free life of her own. Although I never had any problems relating to my Dad, that scene was really so touching and I don't think anyone could watch it without getting emotional.

All fathers and all sons have difficult moments, but the way Geoff and Tim handled and scripted that scene was absolutely marvellous. The generation gap, the experienced father versus the 'green behind the ear' son, the steady patience of the 'Dad' clashing with his impetuous and impulsive 'lad' was magnificent.

Add Chiwetel and Joel's performances and you have a classic master-class in writing and acting. Frankly, the same moment in the musical has the similar effect and every time I've seen the show, I cry. I really cry.

The preview of the film was well received by the audience, but as soon as the credits started to roll, most of them were eager to get off to the party! But it was different for us, suddenly it hit me. The film had been made. The end!

"Let's sit for a while and watch the final credits," Sara said, clearly sharing my feelings. We did, and when the 'thanks' rolled up, again, it was a rare feeling of stark reality.

"Thanks to Steve and Richard Pateman and all at W.J. Brookes." It really brought it home to us. Our story was now a movie; our company shared star billing with Chiwetel Ejiofor, Joel Edgerton, Nick Frost, Linda Bassett, Sarah-Jane Potts, Jemima Rooper and all the cast. For some crazy reason I felt nervous. I was physically shaking.

Then I had to face everybody at the party. "How do you feel?"

"What's it like, having your story on screen?"

"Was it really like that?" All the questions I'd expected, but when they actually came at me like bullets from a machinegun. I really didn't want to answer. It was like an intrusion because, deep down, I was still coming to terms with my own private thoughts.

The date for the World Premiere was set for 5th October 2005. As well as the film, there was to be a charity auction. Sir Elton John was to be involved on behalf of The Terrence Higgins Trust. Celebrities had been invited to design a pair of Kinky Boots to be auctioned off. Lots would be happening on that glittering evening.

The producers were keen that I should be very much part of the proceedings. Two days before the premiere I had to go to London on the train and was met at St Pancras Station by my own driver and taken to The Dorchester Hotel on Park Lane where I had lunch with the main members of the cast.

We then faced the press. That included a broadcast on-line interview with forty regional journalists! Amazingly, questions were fired at me as well as at the stars.

A favourite question they liked to ask Joel was "How do you feel playing Charlie Price when the real 'Charlie Price' is sitting here?" And then they turned to me to ask "Steve, What did you think of Joel playing you?"

Joel invariably said that it was pretty testing, having to play a character based on a real person, when the real person is standing watching you perform! As for me, I thought Joel did a brilliant job!

From the Dorchester we were all taken to the Too2much Club in Soho where Sky News interviewed us where the actual filming had taken place.

From there we went to the Odeon in Covent Garden for a BAFTA question and answer session involving Tim Firth, one of the scriptwriters and Julian Jarrold, the Director of the film. This time I was, thankfully, in the audience.

After all these pressurised press calls, what we needed was a quiet beer, so Chiwetel, Joel and I went off for a drink. For a few precious moments, we were anonymous; no one knew who we were. Not that I'm being starry, but we were, at that time, just three 'ordinary guys' having a beer. It was brilliant!

Then we all dispersed, I went to my hotel in South Kensington. The next day was Premiere Day and it was just as exhausting.

After a very uneasy and restless night's sleep with my mind racing, worrying, getting excited and nervous, eventually morning dawned on the big day; the World Premiere of Kinky Boots. It was held at The West End Vue Cinema, Leicester Square. The whole event was organised with military precision, down to the second. We had to be on the red carpet at 6.30 pm on the dot. It was the biggest red carpet I'd ever seen.

The area was cordoned off. There were convoys of cars for all the members of the cast. Progress up the red carpet was monitored and tightly controlled to gain the maximum press exposure. I was obviously further down the pecking order, but the press were just as interested in me, as they were in the major stars.

Just before entering the cinema, the last interview we had to do was for live TV with Jenni Falconer for her very popular Opening Night Red Carpet Show. She was her usual bubbly self, just as she is on TV. She put me at ease and she was even more gorgeous in real life.

After everyone had arrived we took our seats. There were speeches from the stage and then at 7.30 pm the film started.

Dad had never seen the film and we wondered how he'd take the first five minutes; his 'funeral'! As Charlie dropped the shoe into the grave it hit the coffin and Dad, being Dad and a bit of a comic, let out a loud, "OUCH, that hurt!" I think it was heard by people in a couple of rows round us, but I sank in my seat!

Afterwards we were transferred to the party. It was held rather inappropriately at The Titanic Nightclub! The evening included the auction of the celebrity designed boots and one of Lola's boots from the film, all in aid of The Elton John AIDS Foundation.

As we entered the nightclub my personal press agent grabbed hold of my arm and I was whisked away on a whistle-stop tour of the party for celebrity photo meets, greets and photos for the press. Sara followed on as my own personal photographer, as well as constantly telling me the names of the celebrities I was posing with, as I hadn't got a clue!!

It seemed everyone who was anyone was there. There were British soap opera stars from shows like 'Eastenders', 'Coronation Street' and 'Holby City'. The cast of the film and the backers were joined by anyone else who thought a photo opportunity might help promote the film. I was pulled, pushed and man-handled to get the desired photographic result. All the celebrities were great and very keen to know more about me. I was something of a novelty. I was the guy the film was all about.

Ironically loads of people seemed to think everything in the movie was true and were amazed that much of it was artistic licence. They were asking things like, "How was Milan?" "Do you still see Lola", and "Did you really appear on a catwalk in thigh-length boots and fall flat on your face?"

After about an hour of this media circus I was really hot, sweaty, bothered and in need of a break, when suddenly I was pushed into the arms of a stunning lady celeb. Not only that, but I actually recognised her as the world famous super-model, Sophie Anderton.

I'd been watching her in the jungle programme 'I'm A Celebrity, Get Me Out Of Here' the year before. I must admit I had a bit of a crush on her. She was drop-dead gorgeous; not only that, she was lovely as well. To my horror it was the worst photo the night. We really did look like Beauty and the Beast! She looked fantastic and I, in my sweat-soaked blue shirt that clung to me, looked exhausted, wrung out and ready to drop, while she looked fresh, sexy and glamorous as ever.

By 5.00 am all the celebrations were over; our car was there to take Sara and me back to the hotel. Next morning the car returned to collect us taking us to catch the train.

Once again, I was at St Pancras Station. This was where, all those years ago, the BBC stripped me almost naked to wire me up with microphones and here I was back again, after a red carpet premiere of my story. "How funny," I thought, "This is where it all began; 'Trouble At The Top' the first day of filming for the BBC and here's where the second chapter, 'Kinky Boots, The Movie' ends."

The very next day the film was launched where it was set…in Northampton. We assembled at The Moat House Hotel in the town centre where we had all the regional interviews and press calls to do. Chiwetel, Joel, Nick, Linda, Sarah-Jane and Jemima were all there and local television and radio wanted their precious five minutes!

I'd been given only ten tickets to the London premier, so to have a local premiere in Northampton meant that all my workforce, friends and family could see it. The distributers hired two cinemas in a multiplex close to the hotel and two hundred guests who had had anything to do with the making of the TV programme and the film came along. The Director of the film, Julian Jarrold and I visited both cinemas to give a welcoming speech to all our guests and to thank them for all their support.

It was an impressive evening for all of us; even to this day, people who were there many years ago still say what a thrill it was.

For me, it was the Grand Finale to an epic adventure. Now it was back to life as it used to be; a close family life, the daily routine at the factory and privacy.

Or so we thought!?

"When you reach for the stars, high heels get you that much nearer."
Steve Pateman

XXIII

The Customer is Always Right!

We loved to hear from our customers. They have always been our priority.
After all, without them we'd be nothing. Over the years since 'Trouble At
The Top' and the many shows and shoe fairs we've attended, our customer
base had grown beyond our wildest dreams, and it included a huge variety of
people.

Many of them sought our advice in a kind of 'doctor and patient' relationship.
Some confided in us by revealing the most intimate details of their lives,
experiences and desires. Some even hoped we could help them to achieve
their wildest fantasies. For others, just talking about their fantasies was
fantasy enough!

A regular request was for us to act as 'fashion advisors'. They would ask us
which outfits would go best with which accessories, or what colour or
material would we recommend for certain styles of boots and shoes.

Quite a few actually wanted to come to meet us, face to face. They wanted the
opportunity to see the boots, hold them, touch them and feel the texture.
Buying the boots was, for many, more than just acquiring footwear; it was a
sensual experience.

Our range now included clothing and accessories as well as our famous boots
and customers wanted to try things on to see them for real, rather than just
looking at a picture in the catalogue.

When the factory was in full operation it was inconvenient if members of the
public turned up out of the blue, without an appointment. We decided to
convert the boardroom into our reception area, our showroom and our
changing room all in one, so that we could treat our customers well and make
them comfortable.

Most people rang up in advance to make sure that I was available to see them.
If I was busy, Stan, my Number Two, who had by now met so many of our
clients at shows, would do the honours.

Also willing to help were Rosie and Clarice. They became quite comfortable
taking orders and acting as 'customer advisors'. They loved talking to the
people and the people loved talking to them. It was something about sharing
the female aspect of selling. Occasionally they'd be a little surprised! "You'll
never guess what she asked me!" was quite a regular comment from them.

Now I must make clear that by telling you about some of the incidents that happened, I am not in any way belittling our customers. We never made them feel embarrassed. Indeed, in all these amusing 'happenings' they laughed with us and were, without exception, the first to see the funny side of the situation. If anyone was embarrassed, it was invariably us!

I well remember the day a man from a group of bikers rang. "We do a lot of 'ride-outs' and we love all the leather gear. We saw you on the telly and we'd like to come and try on some of your stuff. If that's possible."

"Of course," I said, "I don't have a problem with that. But to be perfectly honest I think it might be better if you could come on a Saturday morning when the factory is closed and quiet."

He agreed, we set a date and they duly turned up; half a dozen Harley-Davidsons arrived. Some guys were on their own, others came with their girls, but all were wearing their leathers, helmets and dark glasses, looking like the archetypal bikers!

The man who had phoned me took charge of the visit. He was big, masculine, broad and bearded and with him was his girl. She was in skin-tight leather and looked amazing!

I took them into the boardroom and offered them coffee. I gave them all catalogues and left them to make their choices. When I came back the 'leader of the pack' came straight out with it. "I've made my choice, I dunno about the rest, but I want a pair of size seven, black patent PVC thigh length boots." He looked at his girlfriend and they both smiled.

I told them I'd nip down to the storeroom and bring back sizes six, seven and eight; a choice to make sure of a good fit. Back I came with three big boxes and put them on the floor.

"It was size seven wasn't it?" I was just checking.
"Yes, that's right," he replied.
"Great." I turned to the lovely young woman and presented her with a boot. "Do you want to take your jeans off or are you happy to keep them on?" Big mistake. There was a tap on my shoulder.
"Oi, you can leave her alone, the boots are for me, not her." The bloke said grabbing the size seven, black patent PVC, thigh length, 4½-inch high-heeled boot from me.
"I'm SO sorry, I just assumed…" I was so embarrassed. You'd think after all the shows I'd done I'd have learned not to assume anything.
"No worries," he grinned, "I suppose I don't look the type to wear them, do I?"

What could I say but apologise again.

"I really am sorry. Would you like to go somewhere more private to try them on?"
"No, we're all mates here," he said taking off his big leather jacket followed by his steel capped bike boots. I was still uncomfortable after dropping the clanger, when he dropped his leather trousers revealing something I hadn't expected. He was wearing black silky knickers, black stockings and suspenders.

He looked straight at me, "You weren't ready for that either, were you?" as once again my face turned red. They all had a good laugh at my expense.

Nothing fazed them. They were all open, honest and genuine. I, on the other hand, had learned another lesson in how to deal with our wonderful and amazing clients.

My lesson was clear. Was this guy hurting anyone? Did anyone care? Did I have the right to criticise? Should I be shocked? Was he any less a valued customer? The answer to all these questions was a resounding, NO!

Thankfully that episode didn't affect our relationship. They trusted our products, our discretion and us. The group bought a lot of boots, shoes and accessories that day. They became really good, loyal customers, who'd simply ring up and say "You know my size, can I have so and so?"

With so many new customers of all shapes and sizes, we decided that to ensure everyone was fitted with exactly what they wanted, we'd offer a 'made to measure' service.

I worked out that I'd have to take exact measurements, so a personalised pattern could be made. I'd measure round the leg in several key places; I'd mark each point with a felt pen on the customer's leg. I'd also measure the distance between each of the points.

Then we could make a pattern for each customer. We'd charge a one-off payment for making the pattern and then, in the future, we could make anything for them since we had their details on file.

Soon after 'Trouble At The Top' a woman phoned and said,
"I'd like to come and see you. I want a pair of boots made for me because I'm not your normal size."
"That's fine," I told her. It was no problem and I arranged a visit.

"I don't want to come when anyone else is around. Is that OK?" She was quite clear about that. I agreed and suggested she should come on a Saturday morning.

"Thank you for being so kind." I led her to the boardroom. She was lovely, bubbly and excitable!
"It's very difficult for me, you see, being a large size. It's not just the skinny birds that want to look sexy!" She giggled, "I've always dreamed of owning a lovely pair of thigh boots."

"Well," I said, "you've come to the right place!"
"You see, being my size there is nowhere I could go to get them made, then I saw you on TV and, oooh, it was like a gift from above! I can't believe I'm here!" She was clearly very excited to be fulfilling a dream.

I made her some tea and we sat down. I then went off to get a few boots for her to look at. All I wanted at this stage was to make sure the feet would be comfortable and then I would measure her legs. We found a perfect fit for her feet and then came the sensitive part.

"I need to get a 'skin' measurement rather than measuring over your jeans because that wouldn't give me a true fitting. But if you'd rather keep them on, I'll do my best…"
"Good Lord, that's all right," she insisted, "I'll take them off, there's no one around."

So there she was in her undies with me kneeling on the floor with my felt pen in one hand and my trusty shoemaker's tape measure in the other, just like Charlie in the film, measuring Lola for the first time.

"How high up do you want the boots to come?"
"Up to…here, I think." She said placing her finger at the top of her thigh.
"Right." I said marking the spot with my felt pen. Then I began to take measurements round the ankle and up to the calf and so on. As I got past her knee she giggled. "Oh, I hate my legs, sorry they're so fat."
"Don't be silly," I said, "Just think, when you get these boots on you'll look so glamorous, you'll feel like a million dollars."

I took all the measurements until I reached her thigh. Now what I haven't told you is that the tape measure I was using isn't like a dressmaker's tape, it's a pattern-cutter's tape designed for measuring knee-length boots!

So when I reached her thigh, my short tape measure wasn't long enough to go round. I didn't have a proper dressmaker's tape with me. I was beginning to panic. She realised what was happening and burst out laughing.

"Don't worry love," she cackled saucily, "My legs, my fault. I bet that's a first for you!"

Thank goodness she saw the funny side. I couldn't start searching the building for a tape and the only other one we had was a metal expandable one with a spring retraction. It was freezing cold steel and it had sharp edges. I wasn't prepared to inflict an injury on such a valued customer!

Brainwave! Improvise! I spotted a pack of bootlaces, ripped open the paper sleeve and unfurled the bootlace. Perfect. I measured it round her thigh, marked it with the felt pen and then measured the bootlace with my shoemaker's tape. Problem solved!

"Well done, Steve." She clapped her hands just like an excited schoolgirl! "Nice to know you have a tool for every job."

A few weeks later she returned to collect her made to measure boots. She was over the moon; she loved them and thought she looked fabulous. She had a tear in her eye as she paraded up and down the boardroom looking in the long mirror at her legs from every angle.

I don't think I've ever seen anyone so happy. She had never in a million years thought she'd own a pair of boots like these because of her size, but together we'd overcome all obstacles and fulfilled her ambition, her fantasy, her dream. Seeing her so thrilled made me feel emotional too.

Once again the boots had worked their magic.

However, not every customer gave us warning of his or her arrival! I remember one young guy turning up out of the blue. He apologised for not phoning in advance, but since he was here, I felt I couldn't send him away. He was a very smart businessman, well dressed and groomed, carrying a large kit bag.

"I was just passing and I hoped I could look at some of your boots." It was obvious he was a bit uncomfortable not having phoned first, "Is that all right?"

What could I say? "Yes, of course, come on up." I took him to the boardroom. "Sorry we are a bit strapped this morning, but if you can bear with us, I'll get someone to come and help you."

I gave him some catalogues and left him looking through them. It really was a busy morning; Rosie told me a couple of suppliers had phoned and asked me to call them back urgently. After making one of the calls, I remembered the poor guy I'd left alone. I phoned down to Stan.

"There's a guy in the boardroom looking at catalogues, can you see if he's OK? I'd forgotten all about him. If you can sort him out I'd be grateful. Rosie or Clarice will help if you need them."
"Did he have an appointment?" Stan obviously didn't want to be disturbed either.
"No, but I couldn't turn him away," I said, "he seems like a nice guy. Can you check on his size and take a few samples up to him?"

Stan said he would and I carried on with another phone call. About ten minutes later Stan came up and popped his head round the door.

"Steve," he said quizzically, "that bloke, where did you put him?"
"In the boardroom where I always do." I whispered with my hand over the telephone receiver, "Why?"
"He's gone."
"What d'you mean, he's gone?" I knew he must be there.
"Gone!" Stan said firmly.

"But I left him there." I put my hand up, "hang on a minute, Stan."
I went back to the phone and asked if I could call them back in five minutes and hung up.

"Stan, you're joking." I got up and went to the door. "Let's go and see."
As we started up the stairs, Stan said, "There's a woman in there, did she come with him?"
"A woman? No, he came on his own." I was flummoxed.

We both crept up to the boardroom and lightly tapped on the door and as it creaked open we saw a stunning young woman standing in front of the mirror.

She turned quickly, "Steve, I hope you don't mind, but I had all my things with me and when I put my skirt on I couldn't resist putting my wig and everything else on too. I hope it didn't give you a shock."

"No," I said, "that's quite all right. Let's get you fitted with the boots to complete the outfit." I gave Stan a stare, shook my head and left the confused Stan to it.

It was a remarkable transformation; she looked fabulous. She was so thrilled with the boots; she couldn't stop parading up and down the boardroom. Stan completed the sale and he left her still admiring herself in the mirror as she reluctantly made the transformation back.

I just happened to be passing close by when Stan and our customer, now once again the smart young businessman, were saying their goodbyes. Stan was still apologising profusely for the earlier confusion while the young guy was laughing it all off. After all, he was happy. He was clutching his newly acquired boots.

We always tried to make our boots 'fit for purpose', but sometimes we weren't always sure what 'the purpose' was! One woman had ordered some thigh length boots with a full-length inside zip and seemed really pleased with them. Then, some weeks later, she phoned to make a small complaint.

"What's the problem?" I asked; always keen to keep the customer happy.
"Well, you may remember I wanted the boots so I could wear them in bed with my husband, and while we were…you know, having…"
"Yes, I think I understand." Spare me the details, I thought. "But what's the problem?"

"Well, the boots are fantastic and just what we wanted, but while we were in our, let's call it, favourite position, the zip kept catching the sides of his rib cage and making him ever so sore and he's got terrible blisters and scratch marks."

I wondered what this 'favourite position' was. What really happened? I might never know!

"I see," I said, "but that's not a manufacturing problem." I didn't know what else to say.
"Oh no," she panicked, "the boots are fine, but I wondered if we could have some made with zips that only come up to the knee, then that would spare his sore sides, bless him."

Always willing to oblige, we made some more boots for her just as she'd asked, with zips up to the inside of the knee and with a bit more padding and soft linings at the top. This would make them more 'hubby proof'.

As so often happens with so many of our loyal customers, we'd met this particular couple later at one of our shows. While Stan was showing her another pair of shoes, the husband came up to me and apologised about his wife's complaint although it had done him a massive favour because it spared him from further injuries!!

Nothing was too much trouble for our 'Divine' customers!

Whenever I've visited exhibitions up and down the country I've always been on the lookout for new lines to add to our catalogue. The 'Erotica' shows always had 'novel' items, but we also realised that the tattooing conventions and exhibitions were also worth visiting because the people who went to them would also like the products we sold.

Although I was going to these shows as an exhibitor, I was also going as a buyer. It was really important that I kept up with innovations and new products. Due to our new-found fame it was extremely important for us to be at the forefront of 'erotic fashion'.

So when I saw something that would fit in with out products, I asked the supplier if we could include it in our catalogue.

One of the products that I'd found at such an exhibition was something called a 'Fun Swing™'. It's hard to describe it, but basically it is what it says on the box! It's on springs, it has harnesses and it bounces up and down, moves side to side and also can swivel nearly three hundred and sixty degrees while it's in use.

It obviously has height restrictions because it has to be fixed to the ceiling by a large eye-bolt that is attached to a rafter, so it would be OK for an average height room. One man had purchased a 'Fun Swing™' from our catalogue. Some time afterwards he phoned in with a complaint. Clarice took the call. She couldn't quite make out what the customer was trying to explain as she'd never seen how it fitted together. So she put the call through to me.

"I'm sorry to hear you have a complaint. Let me see if I can help you. What seems to be the problem?" I was usually ready for anything, but on this occasion even I was taken aback.

"I bought a 'Fun Swing™' from you and I read all the instructions, but I can't get it to work properly. It sort of, well, gets stuck." He was trying to explain, but I still couldn't quite work out what he meant.
"How do you mean, get's stuck?" I wondered if the joints had seized up or the spring had been broken or stretched.

"It doesn't bounce," he volunteered.
"Does it have clearance? Is it off the floor?" I was intrigued. "How high is the ceiling in your house?"
"Well it's not actually in a house."
"Oh, OK. Where do you live then?" I was getting warmer, I hoped!
"I live on a canal boat, a barge."

I couldn't quite believe what I was hearing. A barge? With a low roof? You probably can't even stand up straight, let alone install a 'Fun Swing™', I thought.

"Well, I think that's the problem then. I'm sure it can't have enough clearance. The instructions should tell you the minimum amount of clearance you need. But I'm really sorry, as you've used it already, I'm afraid I can't take it back." I said, defending my rights as a trader.

"Oh I don't want to get rid of it," he said, "the wife loves it, I just wondered if you could supply a smaller spring so we could carry on using it on our boat without bashing our bums on the deck and our heads on the roof."

A vivid picture filled my mind of a sexy Benny Hill sketch! Well, as I keep reminding myself…it takes all sorts!!

Sometimes our customers turned out to be our inspiration! I well remember I was talking to a dominatrix at a show. She was taking great pleasure in explaining how she carried out her role and to whom. But she admitted she had a problem. She kept putting her whip down at the most inopportune moments and losing it in the dark.

"I know what you need," I said, "you need a slender pocket on your thigh length boot. Imagine how sexy that would look as you slowly slide your whip in and out of the pocket. It would always be to hand and you'd never lose it." "I love it!" She said excitedly, "Not only that, but my clients would like it too."

So with a chance meeting and a conversation between the two of us, we designed the first ever 'whip boot', which became an iconic part of 'Kinky Boots', the film and the musical.

Time is never wasted with good customers. They can inspire new designs, lead you to new heights and, treated well, can be the best advertisement you could ever have. Without our customers, the Kinky Boot factory would never have made it to the silver screen.

Kinky Boots premiered in London and was showing in cinemas across the country and in countless towns and cities all around the world.

Kinky Boots just went global!

"Kinky Boots and shoes are just items of footwear until worn by their owner and then they come alive."
Steve Pateman

XXIV

Victim of My Own Success!

After the TV programme, the film, all the shows and exhibitions we'd been to, we had a couple of years of really good trading. We'd found our 'niche market' and quickly earned a reputation for good service and exceptional products.

But success had a price. At one of the Düsseldorf shows we'd met an English guy who really showed a great interest in the 'Divine' range. He talked to us on the stand, asked questions about the production process and became something of a regular visitor. We thought he was a genuine buyer.

Later we found out he was a wholesaler from Leicester and his interest was entirely professional on his part. He was 'grooming' us to find out as much as he could with a view to making a 'fast buck' out of the Kinky Boot market.

A few months after the show I had a phone call from one of the shops we supplied. The manager of the shop had just received a call from a wholesaler in Leicester claiming to be the main supplier of Kinky Boots in the UK. Fortunately for us, the manager who'd received the call was rather suspicious, because he knew that we'd have contacted him if we had changed the way were supplying our goods.

Our customer gave us the phone number of the rogue supplier and I gave him a ring. Lo and behold! It turned out to be the guy who'd shown so much interest in our boots at the Düsseldorf show.

Being well off, he'd decided to throw a load of money into buying cheap Chinese imitations of our boots and shoes and was selling them at the same price that I could make them for. He was trying to flood the market with poor quality, poor fitting, terribly designed and shoddily made boots and shoes at half the price of ours.

From being a genuine manufacturer and supplier, we were now faced with opposition from this man selling cheap and very inferior footwear.

Thankfully, our regular customers stayed loyal to us, but within the Kinky Boot and shoe business there are always a lot of 'one off' customers, who want a pair of boots for a party or whatever, and naturally they would go for the cheap imitation.

It turned out that this man was one of many who popped up in the imitation business and they were gradually killing the trade that we'd built up. For years we'd been fighting cheap imports in our original range of W.J. Brookes footwear, and we'd overcome that by introducing the 'Divine' range; BUT now it was happening all over again.

We'd become the victim of our own success. Despite still having the premises in King Street, next door to our factory, regular customers were still coming to buy from us, but these were getting fewer and fewer as the months went on.

All this had an incredibly serious effect on me. Having been the boss of a successful factory with eighty employees, a three-storey building and a thriving mail order business, I was used to running around, being busy, being useful. Now suddenly I was almost imprisoned in a small office with only a cramped warehouse to walk round, I was beginning to feel like a caged lion. I was frustrated and this is when I started to consider changing the direction of my life once again.

One day I happened to hear an item on the local radio station; it was about recruiting retained firefighters. It sounded interesting to me; challenging, worthwhile and exciting. I made contact and learned I could become a Retained Fire-fighter in my home village of Earls Barton while still continuing with the business.

I'd have a 'pager' to alert me to action when I was on call. I would then have to drop everything and get to the fire station, jump on the fire engine and go off to a fire, a road accident or any other emergency that had arisen.

It sounded a perfect solution to my frustration. A new lease of life. I still had Stan and Clarice working with me and I could trust them to keep the business on track if I was called out.

I passed all the entrance tests to become a Retained Fire-fighter with Northamptonshire Fire and Rescue and enjoyed it so much that I considered doing the job full-time. To become a whole-time fire fighter involves a long, hard process of physical and written exams, with thousands of applicants, so there's just a little bit of competition!!

I first tried with Luton and Bedfordshire Fire and Rescue Service and I was successful along with thirty others, at which point I was placed on a year's waiting list.

Being rather impatient, not wanting to wait, I applied to Staffordshire Fire and Rescue. I went through the same process again as I had with Luton and

Bedfordshire Fire and Rescue and again, luckily, I made it all the way through to the interview stages. Having had what I thought was a really good interview it was again, a 'fingers crossed' waiting game. I waited patiently and decided that if I didn't hear soon I'd settle for being just a Retained Firefighter.

Then out of the blue I was accepted by Staffordshire and later on the same day, I was accepted by Luton and Bedfordshire. It was just like waiting for a bus. None come for hours then two come along together! I couldn't believe it! Now I had to make a choice, which one to go for? To go south? Or to go north? Eventually I decided on north. For many reasons it seemed to be a better choice for me.

I felt I was really lucky to be accepted. The recruitment process was very complicated and I was one of about 5,000 initial applicants. Then they filter the numbers down through written application forms to half that number and then there are tests and interviews. I felt proud at the ripe old age of 43, to be starting a new career doing something I loved.

Life as a full-time firefighter took all of my time, which meant my commitment with 'Divine' became less and less. Eventually, I had to make a decision. Frankly, the decision was made for me. The orders were in decline. Cheap imports were undercutting sales. Although it was something I loved, my heart was no longer fully in it.

Everything seemed to be against me yet again. This time I wanted to come out on top; I had achieved what I'd set out to do…and more!

Sadly, 'Divine' had to close. I wasn't going to allow anyone else to take over my 'baby'. I'd given it my all for so long and to sell the business on to a complete stranger was unthinkable. So I had to do, once again, the thing I hated most. I had to face telling Stan and Clarice that I was closing the business and they'd be losing their jobs. It was heart-breaking for all three of us, but they knew. They'd been with me through thick and thin and realised the writing was on the wall.

I was no longer a bootmaker. A new door had once again opened. After completing twelve weeks of training, I started my first shift at Lichfield Fire Station and a great team of fire fighters helped me through my probation to become a fully qualified firefighter.

But living away from home for ten days in every fourteen was hard, so eventually I managed to transfer back to my home county, where I first started my career, as a retained firefighter. I was posted to Mereway Fire

Station in Northampton. Being back at home was so much better for the family and for me.

Another new chapter had started. Being part of a technical rescue team, swift water rescue, boat rescue, as well as firefighting, gave me yet more skills to learn.

Would this be my last big change?

Would there be anything else to add to the story? Who knows what the future holds for us?

Often people ask, especially when I do my after dinner talks, "Which would you rather be doing? Shoe making or firefighting?" It's an extremely hard question to answer. Shoes have been my life, my history and my inspiration. They have given me amazing opportunities and a journey into a world I never knew existed.

But as much as I would love to be back in the footwear trade, manufacturing nowadays must be so hard in this country. Limited suppliers of components, dwindling skills, production costs, red tape and even more legislation; I just don't know how the existing companies manage to do it. I take my hat off to them. I applaud them.

My new career operationally as a firefighter is dynamic, exciting and challenging. Helping those in trouble is both humbling and very rewarding. But on the other side, working as a public servant nowadays with all the cost cutting, reduction in staff and the constant change for change's sake is very demoralising for all who work in the emergency services.

Life in the shoe factory is now history for me; it can never be again. My story so far has been all about taking risks, going forward, not dwelling on the past. It's all about looking for the next great adventure.

As I write, I have five years left as an operational firefighter, having to retire at the age of 60. Then I will have to find some useful way of filling the next seven years until I can draw my old age pension at the grand old age of 67. A new working career? Who knows how I will fill those years? Life is an 'open book' and one yet to be written!

"A niche market can bring success, but it also brings new problems and challenges."
Steve Pateman

XXV

The Back Streets of Barton to The Bright Lights of Broadway

It's impossible to compare the difference between life as a full-time firefighter and life as Northamptonshire bootmaker! From being in a Victorian factory with a fairly regular daily routine, to being out in the open air, dealing with real life human dramas is like comparing chalk and cheese.

My new life is exciting, challenging and sometimes dangerous, but every day is different and I never know what the next shift will bring.

What's more, although my colleagues knew all about 'Trouble At The Top' and the film that followed, that part of my life doesn't impinge on my new career. In fact, once I'd immersed myself in my new career, I hardly thought about it.

Until another phone call brought it all to the surface again.

The call came from Nick Barton of Harbour Pictures. "Steve, I thought I'd let you know, we've just heard they're thinking of making Kinky Boots into a musical."

"Oh dear," I thought. "That was then, this is now." Perhaps I was getting cynical and jaded, but what occurred to me first was, how many musicals are planned and never get made. However, as the weeks and months went on, we heard more about the plans. Then came the big news that Cyndi Lauper was to compose the music and that sounded exciting.

In my early days I'd been a DJ in night clubs and had my own disco and I'd played Cyndi's hits like 'Girls just wanna have fun' over and over again. WOW, if someone that famous was on board, maybe the musical had a chance.

But it's my story; no one had contacted me; that made me feel a bit strange. After all, Charlie Price was modelled on me; surely, being based on my true story, I could be of use to them? Unfortunately, that wasn't the case.

They'd secured the rights to make the musical from the Disney Corporation who held them. I quite understood, but I still felt I should have been consulted. Of course I was disappointed and upset at the lack of contact, but at the same time, thrilled that the musical could be made.

It all started in 2006 when Daryl Roth, the ten-times Tony Award winning Broadway producer, saw the film 'Kinky Boots' at the Sundance Festival and thought it would make a brilliant musical. So in 2008 she started to put plans together. She made a deal with the Disney Corporation, owners of the rights. In 2010 Harvey Fierstein and Cyndi Lauper joined in as writer and composer.

It was clearly going to be something big. Surely there would be some way I could be involved? So I found out who was promoting the show and I emailed them.

'My name's Steve Pateman,' I wrote, 'I'm the man the character Charlie Price in the film is based on. I'm so pleased you're going to make a musical. I'd love to be part of it, not in any financial sense, but I'd love to come to the premiere. If you could give me a couple of flights and tickets for the show, put me up in a hotel for the night and give me a couple of beers, I'm yours. You could use me for whatever promotion you want; personal appearances, interviews, you name it, I'm your man.'

The response was less than enthusiastic. 'We'll think about it,' was the nearest to positive they offered, 'if you can get yourself here and find your own accommodation, we'll give you a couple of tickets for the show.'

Big deal! I didn't go. Do I regret it? Yes, I suppose I do in many ways; but then again, I now had another job, my life was very different. Could I afford the flights and a Manhattan Hotel? Frankly, no!

I would have loved to have been there, but who knows, I might have been seen as a hanger-on, out of place, just another 'stage door groupie' hidden in the corner. It could have been a complete waste of time and money.

At the time it was a very bitter-sweet pill to swallow and even to this day, I'd love to go to New York to see the show, because that's where it started. But I've moved on; the show has moved on. I've seen it several times in London and I'm extremely proud of it. But I'd have been even more proud if I'd been part of the opening night.

The pre-Broadway run was in 2012 at the Bank of America Theatre, Chicago and was an instant hit. A year later on 3 April 2013 it opened at Broadway's Al Hirschfeld Theatre. It opened to luke-warm reviews.

At the same time the British show, Matilda the Musical had opened to rave reviews. It was approaching the 'award' season, and a month after opening Kinky Boots was easily beating Matilda in the audience stakes.

The nominations for the Tony Awards were released. Kinky Boots had more than any other show; a staggering 13 nominations. On the night it won 6 out of the 13; including Best Musical, Best Original Score and Best Choreography. The cast recording instantly went to number one on the Billboard Cast Albums Chart.

A story about a small Earls Barton bootmaker had swept the board on Broadway! It was unbelievable, and I wasn't there.

As it turned out, one of our best friends, Vicky, went to New York and saw Kinky Boots. She brought me a programme, known as a playbill on Broadway, and a CD of the cast recording and she went round to the stage door and got some of the cast to sign the programme.

As soon as she gave it to me, I searched through and there wasn't even a mention of my name. "Based on a true story" was the nearest it came to identifying me. Couldn't they even have added, "...of Steve Pateman"? That would have meant a lot to me.

But time is a good healer. I've followed the musical's progress closely and I'm thrilled at its success. I know what I've done, what I've achieved, so that's all that matters. If people are keen enough to look Kinky Boots up on the internet they'll soon see my name there!

My excitement came by sharing other people's experience of the Broadway production. Mark, Tracy, Liz and Colin, some more of my friends, went over to New York on holiday and made a point of seeing Kinky Boots.

"Try to do what Vicky did," I said, "go round to the stage door and make yourself known and tell them you're friends of the original Charlie Price!"

This they did. They saw the show and loved it, they went to the stage door and told the Stage Door Keeper who they were and about their connection with me, the original Charlie Price. While they were explaining, Adinah Alexander, one of the cast, who played two parts: the role of Trish and also the Stage Manager in Milan overheard and went slightly crazy with excitement. "Oh my goodness, that's fantastic. Wait here I must tell the gang."

With that she disappeared for a few moments and returned with some other cast members and the Stage Manager. They were equally enthusiastic and were asking all sorts of questions about the real 'Charlie' and about the Kinky Boot factory.

The Stage Manager gave them a tour of backstage, showed them the props and the mechanism behind the famous conveyor belt on which one of the most exciting dance routines takes place! After the tour, Adinah told them they were having an after show party and invited them along.

Later, in Adinah's, own words…

"One of my favorite things in a Broadway run is exiting the Stage Door and signing Playbills for the fans who have waited to see us after the show. It's a chance to connect and it means so much to them.

One night I was signing and I heard a voice say "we're from Northampton!!! We know the REAL Charlie Price!" I stopped dead in my tracks and saw Colin and his lovely wife with another couple. I motioned them around the barricade and brought them backstage for a special tour and then we all went to Beer Culture next door for some beer and whisky. We stayed in touch through Facebook and when I posted that I was going to London they invited me to Northampton for the day. They asked what I wanted to do and I said "Meet the real Charlie Price".

They showed me all around Northampton, the Shoe Museum, the Tricker's Factory which is the model for our set. Then we went to the pub to meet Steve!!!! He was so charming and fun and I understood how a man like that could turn his factory into a place where people could buy kinky footwear!!!

He was open and warm and showed me all around Earls Barton, all the places where the film was shot.
It was the highlight of my trip to England and it infused my performances with a richness from seeing all the places that I was pretending to know nightly!!!!

Kinky Boots has been an incredible gift in my life!!!

Thanks Steve!!!

When they came home, they told me all about their wonderful time. I must admit I was jealous (in a friendly way) as, after all, I had still not seen the musical as it was on only in New York.

Adinah became a good friend through this encounter and when she came to England for a holiday, she came up to Earls Barton to see her four new 'Brit friends'. They arranged for her to meet me and we had a wonderful time talking 'Kinky Boots' for hours!

I showed her the outside of the factory where the story first started.

We went to the churchyard where the scenes in the film were shot. She was over the moon as we sat in the same place as 'the Prices' had, on the church wall looking down over the village. I was in awe of her, a Broadway star here in Barton, and she was even more in awe of us and all we showed her.

Somehow my friendship with Adinah, which has become very strong now through our contact on Facebook, has softened my sadness at not being involved in the Broadway show.

Then came the news that Kinky Boots was to be produced in the West End. That was really exciting and raised my profile all over again. As before, I wondered whether I'd be involved in some way because no one had contacted me from the London production end.

I needn't have worried. Someone from the Kinky Boots Public Relations Company phoned me with the unbelievable news that they wanted me to be part of it.

In due course they arranged to come up to Earl's Barton to meet me and later I went to London to see them and discuss things further. I was given the date of the premiere and was promised tickets; this time for three of us because Little Dan was now Big Dan at 6 foot 5½, so Sara, Dan and I were to attend as a family.

First though, the PR company invited me to go to a preview of the show at The Adelphi Theatre. That was a day and a half! As well as seeing the show I went backstage and stood in the wings and watched some final rehearsals.

When they had a ten-minute break the PR girls went to see the Director and told him he had Steve Pateman, the original Charlie Price, in the wings. Once again, the reaction was amazing. I went on stage and met the cast and, once again, they fired questions at me.

Killian Donnelly the guy playing Charlie asked the most pertinent question, "Why haven't we seen you before? You'd have been so useful to me to help me form my character." Good point I thought! It was exactly the point Joel had made when I met him on set for the first day of filming.

"How did you feel the first time you met Lola," Killian, asked, "how did the workers in the factory react? What was it like going to Milan?" Questions, questions! It was a real thrill for me and, I reckon, a valuable help for all of them.

The PR girls took me for something to eat and then we went back to The Adelphi for the preview performance. I sat between the two of them. I'd seen a few clips of the musical on-line and I had the CD of the original Broadway cast recording of all the songs, but nothing could prepare me for the experience of seeing the full show live.

The audience comes into the theatre to be met with a painted front cloth filling the whole stage. It depicts our factory with the words, PRICE & SON. BOOTMAKERS. NORTHAMPTON above the door. The auditorium lights go down and Don walks on to warn us to turn our phones off. The front cloth flies out and, wow, the show begins. 'My' story unfolds and for me, it was a roller coaster of emotion.

It's very similar to the film apart from a couple of scenes, but towards the end of Act One, just before the interval, there's a really moving song, 'Not My Father's Son', a duet between Lola and Charlie. In it they share their emotions about their relationships with their fathers and the expectations they have to live up to throughout their lives. That moment truly hit home for me and I started to cry.

It got worse and worse as the song progressed and in the end, I was sobbing my heart out, even though I tried to hide it, I was aware of the PR girls either side of me handing me tissues. I was reliving so much of the story and by the time the lights went up for the interval, I was an emotional wreck!

In many ways I'd detached myself from the story. I'd thought I had closure, but it had opened all the thoughts and memories I'd tried to suppress. My life had been busy and other things occupied my mind. But here it was again. It was my story. In my home country. The story had come home. Where it belonged!

In many ways I was surprised that such an English story had caught the imagination of the Americans and now worldwide audiences. But it is a universal story about emotions that everyone can relate to in some way or other.
Harvey Fierstein, who wrote the script for the stage musical, has written that Kinky Boots is, at its heart, the story of two very different men and their relationships with their fathers as they struggle with their own identities. That's why that song is so important in the show. I often wonder how many men in the audience feel the same way I did when I first heard that song.

The show took me back to the happy moments and the sad ones; the exciting feelings and the destructive ones. It particularly hit me when I had to relive the terrible time when I had to make the redundancies and of course the elation of seeing my 'Divine' Kinky Boots becoming triumphant.

I loved the show. Everything about it was brilliant and the feeling at the end will stay with me forever. The audience went wild; they stood and cheered while I just sat there surrounded by a sea of ecstasy. After a few moments I felt bad for not standing up so I struggled to my feet, I was shaking all over so I had to sit down again.

The lights came up and one of the PR women said, "So, what did you think?" The other one said, "Are you all right?" they could see my tear stained face and my puffy eyes. "I just need time," I said, so we sat there letting everyone else leave. I didn't want to talk about it, not even with my two tissue-supplying supporters!

Eventually we found a bar and a restorative little 'pick-me-up' and then I was whisked away to St Pancras Station and home to the family. There was so much to share with Sara and Dan, but I wanted to keep quiet about how the show affected me. It was their story too in so many ways; I wanted them to see it afresh and make their own minds up about it.

So once again, on 'premiere day' we had a train booked for us and, once again, I walked the platform at St Pancras Station; the scene of my first encounter with 'fame' through the BBC programme. It's amazing how a railway station has played such an important part in my life.

The only difference was that the station had been entirely reorganised beyond all recognition. It was now, not only St Pancras International with direct trains to all parts of Europe, but also a shopping mall with all the big-name stores.

As soon as we arrived at our hotel, I was handed a big folder with my name on it. It was the schedule detailing every aspect of the premiere. I handed it to Dan; he was now my personal right-hand man!

We went to our rooms. We opened the door to ours and Sara let out a slightly mournful, "Oh, this isn't what I expected. Disaster, look, there's no mirror, I can't make do without a proper mirror."

You'd think the sky had fallen in.

"Let's go and see what Dan's is like," I said, hoping to cheer her up. Dan opened his door. He was over the moon, "Wow, what a room," he beamed, "It's fantastic."

Oh dear, he'd been given our room and we had his. "I don't have to move do I," he pleaded. Sara and I looked at each other and she shook her head. "All right, but the only concession is that we borrow your big mirror." "Done," said a delighted Dan. With that we removed the mirror and made our way back to our room much to the amusement of the other guests as we passed them in the corridor.

After we'd sorted ourselves out and had something to eat in the restaurant, our PR people met us in the foyer and took us to the car that was waiting.

We arrived at The Adelphi Theatre on The Strand and we could see all the crowds gathering and the press waiting in their enclosure. There were roped off areas on the red carpet either side of the main entrance. Most of the other celebrity guests were using the left-hand side, so I started for that with Sara and Dan.

"Just a minute," our PR runner said, "We have to go in on this side." That was the moment when we started to feel like outsiders, we weren't really involved. Cyndi Lauper, Harvey Fierstein and all the 'A-listers' were using one entrance; the also-rans like us, used the other.

We by-passed most of the press. I was a bit disappointed, Sara was spitting feathers, but I didn't want to make a scene, so we went in as directed. We did have some photographs taken in front of the promotional material and we were introduced to a few people as we waited for the real stars to come in.

Then Cyndi Lauper, Harvey Fierstein and the others came in and worked their way down the line shaking hands. It was a like a royal occasion when The Queen spends a split second with each person. When Cyndi reached me, I started to say, "Hi, I'm Ste…" and she'd gone!

The PR runner told us not to worry. They're all like that just before the show starts; the time to mix with everyone would be at the party after the show. We were taken to the Circle Bar for champagne and then we took our seats in the Dress Circle along with all the celebrities.
That made us feel a bit better. Sara, as usual, was looking round to 'spot the celebs' while I sat and relaxed for the first time in ages.

The show started and we could feel the electricity coming from the cast and over the footlights.

Then came 'that' song, the duet between Charlie and Lola that had affected me so much at the preview. It all happened again, the tears and the sobbing. Sara tried to comfort me, Dan was embarrassed, and I was embarrassed because he was embarrassed. What a trio!

During the interval our PR runner introduced us to a few people and then to the actress Michelle Collins who had starred in the British TV soaps 'Eastenders' and 'Coronation Street'. That was a highlight because she seemed to be on her own and so she stayed with us and talked for the rest of the interval!

I popped to the Men's Room before Act Two and I heard some of the comments from other members of the audience. All were favourable; they were clearly enjoying it and one guy even said he remembered the BBC 'Trouble At The Top' programme. "Great," I thought. Then another man said, "But there's nothing about that in the programme." That set my mind going again, someone else had spotted the omission.

I went back to my seat and told Sara about the comments, "Why didn't you tell them who you are?" she said, "they'd have been impressed." Good old Sara, my one-woman publicity machine!

It crossed my mind all the way through the second act. There I was sitting with Sara and Dan, and all these people round me, and not one of them knew that I was the real 'Charlie Price'. I wondered what they'd think if they knew. At the end I whispered my concern to Sara. Big mistake!

As we stood there while others squeezed past us to get out, the guy who'd sat next to me stood up to pass the three of us. "You're a lucky man," Sara said to him, much to the poor man's surprise, "You don't know who you've been sitting next to. Do you?"

I shrank into my shell! "Sorry?" he said, Sara rose to her full height, "he's the real Charlie Price, my husband, Steve Pateman."

Then it was like that moment years ago, on the underground train, when I was recognised by the man sitting opposite. He then told the whole carriage. It was like that all over again. The man next to me in the theatre didn't rush out, he stopped and talked to us and asked all the usual questions. Then others overheard him and joined in, and before long we had our own circle of admirers and they were quizzing Sara and Dan as well as me.

"But there's nothing about you in the programme" one clued-up man commented. Oh dear! I tried to wriggle out of it diplomatically, it wasn't my place to criticise, so I let it pass without saying too much. But it hurt.

The after-show party was held in The De Vere Grand Connaught Rooms not too far from the theatre. We thought we'd be part of the media circus, but we weren't. We met up with Nick, Susanne and Peter from Harbour Pictures, the producers of the Kinky Boots film, and had a good chat.

The party was interesting; Sara spotted some celebrities and dragged me over and introduced me and we also bumped into some members of the original Broadway cast. They were most impressed to meet me and I wondered if they had met my friends Mark, Tracy, Liz and Colin when they saw the show in New York.

With mixed emotions, it was a great party. I worked the room with Sara leading the way, she was better than the bought-in PR people, with her spotting celebrities, hunting them down and cornering them like a lion stalking its prey.

She got me into some great conversations with Graham Norton, Sue Pollard, Sarah-Jane Potts and the cast from the opening night's performance.

We eventually tracked Cyndi Lauper down and introduced ourselves; she spent a few moments with us, surrounded by her bodyguards. We couldn't stand too close to her, we couldn't hold drinks in our hands while we talked to her. It was very regimented. But she did allow me to have a photo with her before she was whisked off.

Was she impressed, having met the real Charlie Price? We'll never know. Had she made Kinky Boots hers? Certainly it's now a world-wide sensation with her name on it. But the story still belongs to Barton.

To those who lived it, worked it; after all, like all stories, I feel we must never forget where it came from and the real people who made it happen.

As well as the awards on Broadway, in 2016 the London production of Kinky Boots won three Laurence Olivier Awards, including Best New Musical.

At the time of writing, 'Kinky Boots The Musical' has played, or is playing, in Chicago, New York, San Francisco, and is on Tour in the USA, Seoul, Toronto, Brisbane, Sydney, Malmo, Tokyo, Hamburg, Manila, Warsaw and London as well as now touring in the UK.

"Accepting everybody's differences makes for a better world."
Steve Pateman

XXVI

As Lola Said,
"Change Your Mind About Someone."

Kinky Boots was part of my life for a good twenty years. In many ways, it's still important; people are still interested in hearing my story and, thank goodness, the film and the musical continue to amuse, entertain and inspire.

Who would ever imagine that an old Victorian factory in the back streets of a small historic shoemaking village in the heart of England would be the subject for two TV programmes, a highly nominated film and a multi-Tony Award winning stage musical?

From the back streets of Barton to the bright lights of Broadway.

The next step would be for the story to be made into a film musical and the set would be complete! Why not? There was a time when virtually every successful stage musical was given the full Hollywood treatment, from ''Show Boat right through to 'The Sound of Music' and 'Legally Blonde'!

It was the TV programme that started it all off, and I thought that was exciting enough. Little did I know that would only be the start of it!

From Barton to Broadway is a long journey and I hope you've enjoyed travelling that journey with me in these pages. Like all journeys mine has been a series of lessons and I sincerely hope that I've learned a lot on the way. Remember, I was brought up in a small town as part of an average family with my father Richard, my mother Margaret and brother Duncan. From Croyland Infant and Junior Schools I went on to Wellingborough School and then straight into the family business at the age of sixteen.

Although my aspirations on leaving school lay elsewhere, circumstances led me into a life of shoemaking; an industry that I took to and developed a passion for. I loved starting the morning with loads of skins of leather and ending the afternoon seeing completed shoes leaving the factory. Every day held a sense of achievement. It was a way of life I never regretted.

It taught me that the smallest opening can lead to great things. So, I believe it's always important to seize every opportunity that comes your way; who knows, it might just change your life!!!

All those years ago, how easy it could have been for me to say "No" to Sue Sheppard of 'Lacies-Fantasy Girl'. It was, after all, a simple business decision. I could have said 'no' because we didn't make women's footwear.

You see I'd never really come into contact with cross dressers, swingers and the kinky industry before. How easy it would have been to have said, "I'm not getting involved with products like that". But thank goodness I did; I've always been intrigued by the unusual, the extreme, loved a challenge and I'll be forever grateful to Sue Sheppard for opening my mind to a new world!

But something inside me said, "Take a chance". If we hadn't taken that chance, braved that new world and taken that truly dramatic step, we would certainly have missed out on the world of red patent leather, high heeled shoes and Kinky Boots!

Millions of followers of my story would never have had the opportunity to see a TV programme, a film and a musical. My hope is that my story has enriched people's lives, changed people's opinions and gained acceptance for so many people around the world.

The thought of taking on a different persona is as thrilling to me as it is, I suspect, to most people. Whether it's dressing up as a hero or heroine, acting out a secret fantasy or simply breaking free from everyday confines is, surely, something we all enjoy in one form or other.

It's so easy to dismiss other people's way of life, their ideas, even their beliefs just because we don't understand them.

Why do people condemn these amazing people? Is it fear? Do they feel threatened? Or are they simply unable to cope with people who aren't like them?

Who are we to judge? Perhaps we should be more open to change. How easy it is to be 'conventional'; there's no challenge in leading a 'normal' life. But it takes great courage to live life as a true individual, to follow a life-style that goes against accepted social conventions, to allow your 'true colours' to shine through.

The only boundaries that enslave us are the ones we impose on ourselves. This is surely a time to say, "forget what anyone else thinks; this is me, this is my life, and I'm going to live it how I want to, where I want to and with who I want to."

I love 'people watching' and these thirty years have given me some wonderful people to watch and learn from.

All the people I've come to know and love have been so open, accepting, trusting and giving. They have welcomed me into a world that I knew nothing about and have shown me a different outlook on life.

After all I've been through, I realise that being blinkered is a terrible thing. My motto has always been, 'Give everything a chance'. If you don't give it a chance, you'll never know what you've missed out on.' I know I may sound like your mother or father, but you'll never know if you'll like something until you've tried it. If you don't like it, you won't have to do it again. If you do like it, give it your best and become your own person.

Do I have any regrets? No! OK, I made a complete fool of myself many times, I've done many stupid things, made mistakes and embarrassed myself beyond belief, but I don't regret it. I want to slide into my grave when the time comes, worn out, exhausted, showing the scars of a full and hectic life. I want to go shouting, 'WOW what a ride!!!"

Shoemakers have been making Brogues, Gibsons, and Oxfords for years, but to make something like our 'Divine' Kinky Boots opened up a whole new world. I just wish I'd found 'Kinky Boots' thirty years earlier when I first started working in the factory; who knows what could have happened by now?

Those boots and shoes have allowed me to meet the most fantastic people. I know not everyone understands their life-style; I didn't at first, but when I did get to know them better everything changed.

When I was invited to visit their clubs, their exhibitions and meetings, I realised that they were just everyday people doing extraordinary things, pursuing their fantasies and enjoying their lives to the full.

I've learned so much about them. The most important thing is that they don't give a damn about other people's opinions. They are who they are. They are proud to be able to stand up and admit it.

So many people lead 'double lives'; never admitting who they really are, how they really want to lead their lives and what they really want to be doing. At the end of the day, they are only cheating themselves and depriving themselves of their true identity.

On the serious side, there was a time when it was almost impossible to buy men's sizes in ladies shoes and boots. So if I have, in some small way through my 'Divine' footwear range, contributed to the happiness of those people who now like to be known as cross-dressers or 'trans', then my life in the shoe trade has been worthwhile.

Think of those people, both male and female, who feel trapped inside their bodies, knowing that they should be the opposite gender. Can you imagine how painful and distressing that must be? Having to live that existence, knowing that the 'inner' self doesn't match the 'outer' self?

The people I've met, whether for biological, psychological or any other reasons feel liberated enough to live their own lives their way. What freedom that must give them!

It's hard nowadays to be entirely non-judgemental because the press and social media somehow manage to influence us, often without our realising it. This is especially difficult for young people who set such store on what they see and hear through Twitter, Facebook and Instagram. With the growth of Fake news, 'touched-up' pictures and the art of Photoshop, people's flaws are being airbrushed out to give that 'false look of perfection'.

These forms of mass communication have a huge influence on the young people of today. If only they could influence them for the better, to make them see that we are all 'average'; we are all insecure; no one is perfect, we all have flaws! We should rise above the opinions of others, especially social media, the bigots and the bullies.

I suppose it's all a question of how we, and others, judge our lives. I look at it like this.

It's like going to a theatre to see your life being played out upon the stage; where you sit is important because it reflects your perspective and how you see your life being played out.

If you sit right up in the 'gods', the cheapest seats, your view is distorted because of the distance between you and the stage. You look down, only seeing the top of the actor's heads, you don't get to see and hear everything that's going on!

If you are in the Royal Box, often the most expensive seats, you only sit there to be seen and to show off. You only see the play from one perspective, a huge part of the stage is hidden from you. You miss some of the action and often the bit you miss might be the most important part of the plot!

If you are backstage, you might hear what's going on, but you can't see the action, because the scenery gets in the way. Even if you peep through a crack you'll only see a distorted glimpse of life's play.

The only true way to see the play is head on, sitting in good seats in the stalls or the dress circle. That way nothing blocks your view of life's play, nothing gets in the way of your seeing, hearing and experiencing what's going on, on the stage. You get a full and rounded view of life's play.

Where do you want to sit and watch life's play? I know where I want to sit; it's where I can experience life to the full so that I can see the full and rounded picture.

If you change places and sit somewhere else, you'd be seeing life's play from a different angle. You might go in to the theatre thinking you'll hate the play, but there is every possibility that when you see, hear and experience the show from a different viewpoint, you might completely change your mind and your outlook on life.

It's the same with people. Look, listen and get the full perspective.

To all who have followed my life's story in Kinky Boots;
Remember…

As Lola said,
"Change your mind about someone."

"Standing tall in high heels gives you a new perspective on life!"
Steve Pateman

XXVII

How Kinky Boots Changed Our Lives

In this chapter I want to share with you the effect that the story has had on so many people who have been part of the Kinky Boots story, from the BBC2 television programme, to the movie and finally to the Broadway musical!

I've been lucky enough to track down some of the people who played key roles in the story from the beginning through to the end. Having asked them how the story has changed their thoughts and their outlook on life, I've been amazed at the wonderful responses that I have received.

Here are some of their comments, starting with the person who, with that first phone call, inspired me to change my 'outlook on life'.

Sue Sheppard
Owner: Lacies-Fantasy Girl, Folkestone, Kent

"I was the person who originally contacted Steve with the idea of making women's shoes and boots for men and cross dressers. I started my shop in 1995 because I knew from first-hand experience (being transgendered myself) discrimination was rife in those days.

It was hard to get and maintain regular employment, especially once it was known I was transgender. So I started Lacies with a long-term unemployment grant. It quickly grew at a time when things were beginning to open up for the transgender and cross- dressing communities.

There were, however, very few suppliers in those days and they found it extremely hard to keep up with demand.

I searched the Internet and came across the British Footwear Association, who then gave me Steve Pateman's number.

I rang him and we had a conversation about his firm possibly making exotic women's footwear, but in men's sizes…

He changed his factory to making footwear for this new market, which was brilliant and helped solve my supply problem.

The rest as they say is history and it still gives me a tingle when I see and hear about Kinky Boots becoming a successful Hollywood film and major musical.
To think it all came about because of a chance conversation all those years ago!"

Love,

Sue.

Michele Kurland
Producer, the BBC 2 series, 'Trouble At The Top'; 'The Kinky Boot Factory'.

My part of your story starts at that time in the BBC Business Documentaries Department when I was a producer on the long running series, 'Trouble At The Top'. It was a series that followed bosses through a changing time or a new challenge in their business.

We were very keen on making one episode about a traditional manufacturing business; the footwear industry was one we had shortlisted to look at. It was important to find a manufacturer that was rooted in the community with generations of families working there. The aim was to reflect the changing face of British Industry and show how such business were coping.

It was an article about you in the Financial Times that brought us to your door. I remember my first meeting with you and being aware of the pressure that you were under.

Having taken over the family business in that dwindling manufacturing climate and a drastic change in the pound meant you had to reinvent yourself to survive. But there was a very strong bond in the team around you and it felt to us that you would give all you could to make it work.

We always looked for a passion for business in our contributors and you certainly ticked that box.

So your decision to design and manufacture women's shoes for men became our story. It was really a way of looking at a much-loved British Industry under threat and your attempt to save it.

At that time my only knowledge of shoes was buying and wearing them! So I was fascinated by the attention to detail that went into the making of your products. Especially when you decided you wouldn't just make women's shoes for men but that they had to be the best.

From then on it was a journey for all of us. I know it took you some time to trust us but I like to think we didn't let you down.

My film crew bonded with you all and we had a lot of hilarious moments. Who would have guessed that all these years later I would daily be passing bill boards in London advertising the 'Kinky Boots - The Movie' and then later the successful musical, both based on our documentary.

I remember the Erotica fair in Olympia and that mad trip to Germany.

I remember trying to persuade you to let us film you shaving your legs!! But you wouldn't agree.

I also remember that great moment of you modelling the boots and shoes for the photo shoot when you couldn't get anyone else to model them for you.

That said it all. You put 100% into trying to make it work.

The documentary was a massive success with over 5 million people tuning in. This was unheard of for a BBC 2 programme at 9.50 on a Wednesday evening! We beat the launch of 'Sex In The City' on Channel 4 in the same slot. The audience watched our documentary and loved you and all you did to try and save the family business. True British spirit.

Best wishes,

Michele.

Robert Lindsay
Actor. Narrator of BBC2 'Trouble At The Top'
The Kinky Boot Factory.

My goodness, what a journey! When I recorded that programme I remember saying to the producers that it would make a great play. Well, it's been a film, a musical and now a book.

CONGRATULATIONS STEVE!

All the best,

Robert.

Nick Barton
Producer of Kinky Boots ~ The Film

Following the transmission of the Documentary on BBC's Trouble At The Top, we all at Harbour Pictures felt that this extraordinary story about your shoe factory, W.J. Brooke's of Earls Barton, could make a stunning film.

We were fortunate that, following on from making Calendar Girls, we had a first look deal with Buena Vista International in the UK (part of the Walt Disney group).

They agreed to back our film and supported us through the long process of development and production.

It was a brilliant journey! We were blessed to have such a great cast and crew and were fortunate that the Pateman family, who owned the original factory, became so involved with the making of the movie.

Highlights for me were the opening Gala Screening of KINKY BOOTS at the Sundance Film Festival with Robert Redford in the audience. And me dancing with Chiwetel Ejiofor at our end of film wrap party in the Soho nightclub!

Little did we know then how KINKY BOOTS would storm onto screens and stages around the world.

Nick Barton.
Chief Executive of Harbour Pictures Productions

Peter Ettedgui
Producer, Kinky Boots ~ The Film

Bringing KINKY BOOTS to the screen was a wonderful experience. I'll never forget my first trip with Suzanne Mackie (one of my fellow producers) to W. J. Brookes, the men's shoe factory, which had been in Steve Pateman's family for three generations.

Steve gave us a tour and introduced us to the staff – his extended family! In the cutting room, we watched spellbound as a veteran craftsman in his overalls stooped over his work-table and precisely cut the curves of the inside leg of a thigh-length boot out of a side of electric red patent leather.

That image, that moment – the juxtaposition of intricate craftsmanship with intimations of the 'kinky' world for which these boots were designed – seared into our minds.

There it was, our embryonic film, in a nutshell.

A few years later, when we finally returned to Northampton to give 'Kinky Boots' a special local premiere, it felt like we were bringing the film home to the proud seat of the British shoe industry where we had spent so much time researching and developing the screenplay. Home to where we had then shot much of the film, at Tricker's splendid Victorian factory, so redolent of Northampton's heyday.

It was at once a sad and inspiring experience – sad, because the industry had fallen on such hard times, with the closure of so many factories, leaving behind the communities and ecosystems that once supported them. Inspiring, because there were people like Steve who were so passionate about keeping the craft and traditions of shoemaking alive in the region, innovating their way out of crisis and finding improbable new markets – such as the iconic Kinky Boots.

Although our film was entertainment, as filmmakers we were infused with Steve's passion and felt like standard-bearers for the region and its fabled industry. Perhaps the nicest compliment I've ever been paid following a film screening came from another shoe factory owner.

He approached me with tears in his eyes after the Northampton premiere, telling me: "Your film has given this city its pride back."

As the film went out into the world beyond Northampton, becoming first an international hit that audiences everywhere took to their hearts, and then Broadway (and the West End) musical, I often thought back to those early visits to Steve and the original 'Kinky Boot factory' – the original inspiration for our project, without whom KINKY BOOTS would never have happened.

Peter Ettedgui.

Suzanne Mackie
Producer, Kinky Boots ~ The Film

I remember vividly director Julian Jarrold and our brilliant, and sadly recently deceased production designer, Alan Macdonald, trying to work out if we should build the shoe factory at our designated film stages at Ealing Studios or if it would be better for us to take over a real shoe factory in Northampton.

Both scenarios presented massive challenges to us both practically, financially and creatively.

The shoe factory in our film was going to be our most important location; it was going to be at the heart of Kinky Boots. But taking over a factory had difficult implications for us; we would have to shut down the shoe operations, lay off staff for a few weeks and generally move in to the premises.

A film unit is an enormous operation; it would be akin to a circus taking over a factory!

We scratched our heads for many weeks about what was best for the film. A shoe factory is in many ways a magical place: straight out of a Brothers Grimm fairy tale.

A sensual place, of sight, sound and smell; where mysterious machines and automated arms pull, push and twirl, noisily and rather gracefully, around and around with balletic precision; with complex conveyor belts disappearing in and out of vision, issuing mysterious strange objects, as they embark on an assembly line of cutting and marking, to stitching and pressing, eventually yielding exquisitely crafted shoes, out of what was a piece of leather!

How on Earth could we do replicate this space?

In the end we chose to take over a real factory in Northampton, and to offer every one of the factory workforce to be part of the film. This was a brilliant outcome for us. Everyone was happy and we were able to depict an authentic world of a shoe factory, in all its beautiful detail. We never looked back.

I remember the day actor Chiwetel Ejiofor first walked into our Kinky Boots factory, dressed elaborately as Lola the transvestite. Chiwetel blasted in with such energy, brilliance and talent and stood side by side the wonderful Joel Edgerton, who played the part of Charlie Price, the Kinky Boots factory owner.

We all looked at each other aghast, we could have heard a pin drop, we knew we had our film.

Best regards,

Suzanne.

Joel Edgerton
Played Charlie Price in The Movie

I'm dead impressed, but not surprised, that the sparkly red thigh-highs and the name 'Kinky Boots' is splashed across billboards and buses all over the world; that Steve Pateman's story has become one of those that has struck a chord and stuck around.

Maybe because it's flashy and fun! One of those 'life is stranger than fiction' tales... but definitely because it is a story that's about acceptance and resilience. It always seemed like a vivid version of The Odd Couple to me. Blue-collar and sequins!

There is also something in that resilience of the little guys versus the corporations and a group bonding together to succeed.

Whenever I see the name Kinky Boots plastered around, I always harbour a little pride that somehow I got to play Steve in the film that kicked it all off.

Then I got to meet him, know him and sit down to hear his stories straight from the horse's mouth. He gave me a pair of the original thigh-high, red patent leather boots with the riding crop on the side. The same style of boots that became the centre piece and masterpiece of Lola in the film and the musical.

I've worn Steve's boots twice since shooting. They now live at my old high school. My mother donated them there, so they are still, as intended, on display.

One interesting note before I finish, as a sign of how Steve's legacy touches people in all sorts of ways: those boots he gave me found their way onto my 80-year-old grandmother one night at a party. She was helped around the room and laughed her old head off. She's gone now. (Don't worry, the boots didn't kill her) but it's always one of the great stories about her that my mother tells.

One of those great moments where someone otherwise conservative just lets themselves go, be a little silly and try something different.

I'm thankful to Steve and for the movie. Still waiting for my call for the audition for the musical though...

Cheers Mate,

Joel.

Sarah-Jane Potts
Played Lauren in The Movie

I was a very new mum to my 6-month-old Buster, just back from working in the States for a good few years. Pretty invisible as an actress back in the UK. No agent, no meetings. Completely overtaken with my new position and not much else. My mobile phone rang.
I didn't usually have time to charge it let alone answer it anymore!
On the line was Gail Stevens the casting director of Kinky Boots.
Our conversation went something like this.

Gail "Is that Sarah-Jane?"
Me "Yes, it is."
Gail "It's Gail Stevens here. Casting director…are you still acting?"
Me "Urm…I think so…"

This is whilst juggling a baby and the phone and the dinner I was making and my interest growing.

Gail "There's a film I'm casting. I want you to read it. I think you're Lauren…"

And then I was Lauren and I found myself in a beautiful and very real shoe factory in Northampton telling the unorthodox tale of love, family, prejudice, humour, honour, bravery and spirit. And I had a ball!

It's funny; I had no idea that Kinky Boots was actually based on a real story until I met Steve and his lovely family in Northampton all those years ago.

It was a pleasure then and it's a pleasure now to make any small contribution to what Kinky Boots was, is and has become. Something that truly makes people smile and feel good.

And as Lauren once said, "Maybe you judge what you leave behind by what you inspire in other people…"

Love,

Sarah-Jane.

Jemima Rooper
Played Nicola in The Movie

Oh God! It was so long ago my poor brain can't really remember! What I do remember is that when I read the script I just adored it - the story - and even though my character wasn't quite as sympathetic as the others I just wanted to be a part of that film. I remember thinking "I'll sweep floors-anything!" I adored working with Joel and Chiwetel. Sarah Jane and Kellie Bright were already mates - it was a bit special. Really though, I wanted to be Lola and I still have my own pair of Kinky Boots that we received on wrap and have since done my fair share of drag roles...it felt like family and that was because of your incredible story!

All the best,

Jemima.

Harvey Fierstein
Playwright and Actor.
Responsible for adapting the story of Kinky Boots – The Movie into The Hit Broadway Musical.

All of us, even in our daily lives, are asked to step out of our comfort zones and take risks. We almost always dismiss these challenges out of hand but, each one of them is actually an opportunity to change the trajectory of our journey. It's so much easier to say "no" but saying "yes" makes life interesting, adventurous and new.

Steve's story is proof that saying "yes" can facilitate miraculous change far beyond our imaginations. Steve not only said "yes" to making boots, but to saving jobs, to opening minds and, let's not forget, that his saying yes has given the world a wonderful movie and inspirational musical theatre piece. I say, "Oi, Oi, Oi" to the power of YES!

Best,

Harvey Fierstein.

Jerry Mitchell
Producer: Kinky Boots - The Musical

Crazy Ideas can sometimes be even bigger than you ever expected. When Steve had the idea to save his factory little did he expect that idea to turn into a film and then a hugely successful worldwide musical. Listen to your crazy ideas!!

All the best, JM.

Eric "Levi" Leviton
Original Broadway Cast Member

My name is Eric Leviton, I've been with the show since the workshop in January 2012, which was one year after my kidney transplant. I was 46 years old at the time and it turned out to be my Broadway debut. I'm a very lucky man, to not only have my junior high school girlfriend donate her kidney to me, but then to be able to live out my dream of being a part of a Broadway show, all because of her being my organ donor and giving me more life to live.

It's been a thrilling journey to be a part of Kinky Boots this whole time and I'm still enjoying it. I still love hearing from people about how much they love the show or how this was the very first Broadway show they've ever seen and how excited they are about the message of the show.

Thanks for reaching out. I wish you all the best with the book.

Until then,

Eric "Levi" Leviton.

Eugene Barry-Hill
Original Broadway Cast

I'm the original Simon Sr. I'm still with the Broadway production since the readings backs in 2012. I was doing Aint Misbehavin' in New Haven CT, when I got the call to audition.

The only reason I auditioned was because of the names Jerry Mitchell, Harvey Fierstein and of course Cyndi Lauper. I'd never heard of Kinky Boots and thought at the time 'what a terrible name for a musical'. What do I know?

I did the Chicago tryout, and was asked to join the Broadway company soon after. There was only one role, the Lola Standby, which needed to be cast in NYC. My companion of 8 years, Timothy Ware, had visited me in Chicago to see the show and he decided he wanted to pursue the Lola cover. I was like "suuuuure honey!"

He got an audition, and thru hard work and diligence, he was hired. So we both became part of the Original Broadway Cast. He went on to perform Lola almost 300 times in the next 3½ years. In 2014, Kinky Boots allowed us the affordability to plan and get married in a beautiful waterside wedding. He left the show August 2016 to go back to school to get his Masters in Writing. He graduates this summer HOPEFULLY!

Several original members are still here after all these years. Some have left and been afforded the chance to come back to their original roles. Kinky Boots is the gift that keeps on giving, and still inspires a lot of joy from our audiences. We have Super-Fans. I entertained one the other night backstage. She has seen us 61 times, and is coming back next month for her 62nd, on her 62nd birthday.

We still have a lot of mileage in these shoes, I mean BOOTS!

All the best,

Eugene Barry-Hill.

Ellyn Marsh
A member of The Original Broadway Cast for Six Years.

Many years ago I was doing a show out of town in Kansas and I had offered to babysit my friends' children so that they could have a date night out. When they came home they told me they saw this adorable independent film called "Kinky Boots". I vividly remember them describing the story to me and thinking what a cute idea. They then went on to say it was loosely based on a true story; I thought how inspirational and heart-warming. I had then seen bits and pieces of the movie on various movie channels over the years.

When I heard through the grapevine that it was going to be turned into a Broadway musical I remember thinking how it would musicalize brilliantly. Little did I know that the story would have such a strong message of love and acceptance and of course how this story would play such a huge part in my life.

Originating a Broadway show is a huge honor and nothing short of a bucket list event in a Broadway performer's life; but being a part of a musical a special as "Kinky Boots" is just the sweet cream on top of that sundae.

When Jerry Mitchell introduced all the characters that would make up the factory, some were fictional and some were based on people that he met at the factory in Northampton. Mine, specifically, which I named Gemma Louise, was based on this rock 'n' roll lady with tattoos and a mullet. Jerry was instantly intrigued by her look and said she would definitely make it to the musical and I'm so lucky that I got to portray her on stage; just seeing pictures of her I gathered her essence of a no-nonsense lady with the quick dry wit.

Creating a character that isn't part of the plot is essential to making a show come alive, so it's a lot of backstory we create ourselves; however her exterior look gave me so much to spring board off, that it was very easy (and hilariously fun) to create the world of Gemma Louise.

In the musical we made up our lives in the factory. Many of us had friendships that we had created in order to create this world of the factory that we lived in day in and day out. Lines create a story but the specificity in what everyone is doing creates the world for an audience to be part of for two and a half hours.

Stark Sands was our original Charlie Price and Andy Kelso replaced him and then became the longest running Charlie Price on Broadway. Both of them brought a vulnerability and a sweetness, but also a feeling of being scared out of their minds at taking over their father's factory. They were brilliant leaders of our story.

We were never really sure what parts of the story were true and what parts were added for dramatic effect, but we definitely treated the story as if it had all taken place. When we were performing in the musical many of us in the factory revered Lola as our saviour; as the one who would save our pay checks, our jobs, and our beloved factory.

I have no idea if the people at the actual factory loved their jobs as much as we did, but I certainly hope they did. I love telling the story for six years on Broadway it's been one of my truest honours.

The story on which "Kinky Boots" is based, is one that celebrates the human spirit. That thinking outside the box can sometimes change your life direction; that going against the norm is ok and sometimes the only way; that when we are challenged with failure we can create our own successes.

It's no surprise we have run so long on Broadway, the story and the messages sneak up on you most importantly; you change the world when you change your mind. This simple message has kept this story alive and I love it.

Thank you for sharing your story Steve, I hope we have made you proud!

Ellyn.

Steve Berger
Original Broadway Cast Member

I play "Mr. Price" on Broadway. I originated the role and am still playing it.
As an actor of 'a certain age', I often play characters whose first name is
"Mr."! I watched the movie and freeze-framed the funeral to see that on the
casket, Mr Price's first name is actually HAROLD! Good luck with the book.

My father was also in the shoe business. He started out as a salesman for a
wholesaler and later became a buyer, which involved many trips to Milan and
Asia.

I did the show, but on the first day of rehearsal, I entered the room and the
smell of hundreds of brand new shoes hit me like a ton of bricks. I was
instantly back in his showroom. Also, I spent two summers working in the
warehouse - more smells of leather.

Best,

Stephen Berger.

Adinah Alexander
Original Broadway Cast Member
(see Chapter XXV)

"Kinky Boots has been an incredible gift in my life!!

Thanks Steve.

KINKY BOOTS

Fact and Fiction

FACT:
The original shoe factory was called W. J. Brookes Ltd.
FICTION:
In the film and the musical, it was Price & Sons Ltd.

FACT:
W. J. Brookes made men's and unisex high fashion footwear, traditional styles and, eventually, Kinky Boots for men and women.
FICTION:
Price & Sons made only traditional footwear and then Kinky Boots.

FACT:
W.J. Brookes was run by Steve Pateman. He took over from his Father, Richard, who, as we write is still very much alive!
FICTION:
Price & Sons was run by Charlie Price who took over following the sudden death of his Father, Harold.

FACT:
While in his mid-thirties, Steve Pateman, being a bit of an exhibitionist, is one of those people who, when he hears about a fancy-dress party says, 'Let's go for it, what can I do to shock people'.
FICTION:
Charlie Price, a man in is late twenties, is a bit confused, conservative, traditional and naïve.

FACT:
Steve Pateman is a married family man with a wife Sara and a son Dan.
FICTION:
Charlie Price was not married, but had a fiancée, Nicola.

FACT:
W. J. Brookes began to experience loss of sales due to the high value of the British pound resulting in a downward trend in the Company's export trade and having to fight off cheap imports which caused a loss of orders.
FICTION:
Price & Sons lost money due to losing a contract to their biggest customer and having to complete orders that were in production with no end customer.

FACT:

Steve Pateman came across the idea of Kinky Boots and shoes from a phone conversation with a potential new customer.

FICTION:

Charlie Price came across the idea after an encounter with Lola, a drag queen from London.

FACT:

Steve Pateman was the driving force designing and putting into production his range of Kinky Boots and shoes with the help of in-house designers and staff.

FICTION:

Lola was the driving force for the range of Kinky Boots and shoes and did all the in-house design and Charlie rather took the back seat.

FACT:

W.J. Brookes and Steve promoted their 'Divine' range of Kinky Boots and shoes at Düsseldorf, the largest footwear fair in Europe.

FICTION:

Price & Sons and Charlie promoted their range of Kinky Boots and shoes in Milan.

FACT:

Steve Pateman shaved his legs, learned to walk in Kinky high-heeled shoes and boots and modelled them for a photo shoot for their 'Divine' catalogue.

FICTION:

Charlie Price modelled the Kinky Boots on a catwalk in Milan.

FACT:

W. J. Brookes was saved by Kinky Boots for some years before finally finishing production. Steve Pateman then went on to become a whole-time firefighter.

FICTION:

Price & Sons was saved by Kinky Boots after their success at the Milan Footwear Show and they continued to make Kinky Boots. Charlie broke off his engagement to Nicola and, we suspect, his romantic attachment to Lauren continued to blossom.

Vintage Picture of W. J. Brookes Ltd
Early 1900s

'Divine' Office
Steve, Stan, Clarice and Dad Richard

Steve Testing Out the First Men's
'Divine' Red Ankle Boots
in the Factory.

The First Ever
Kinky Boots and Shoes Sold
It Made the Front Page of a New
London Catalogue

Jane. Our 'Divine' Model

The Original 'Divine' Whip Boot
As Featured in the Film and Musical

'Divine' Photoshoot

The 'Boss in Boots and Shoes'

Steve Pateman Struts his Stuff!

Trouble at the Top

THE KINKY BOOT FACTORY

WEDNESDAY 24th FEBRUARY

9.50pm

BBC2

Series Editor: **Robert Thirkell**
www.bbc.co.uk/education

BBC TWO

Trouble at the Top

Series Producer
Sue Bourne

From the award-winning team behind BBC2's "Troubleshooter", "Back to the Floor" and "Blood on the Carpet", six more tales following top bosses on the roller-coaster of business life.

THE KINKY BOOT FACTORY

WEDNESDAY 24th FEBRUARY 9.50pm BBC2

Shaving his legs and learning to walk in six inch stiletto heels are just two of the things Steve Pateman is doing to save his family business. For four generations the Patemans have been making traditional men's footwear, but a strong pound and cheap imports have taken away his customers. He's convinced his father that making thigh length boots and high heel shoes strong enough for 15 stone men is the answer.

We follow Steve and his family as he puts together his first fetish shoe collection. To survive, he must beat off the competition and get enough orders by Christmas or the 100 year old Northamptonshire company will have to close.

Film Editor	**John McAvoy**
Producer	**Michele Kurland**

BBC TWO
Business and Adventure Unit, Science Department
0181 752 4391

'Erotica' Exhibition at
Olympia in London

Dusseldorf Stand (two pictures above)

Amsterdam Photo Shoot at the Casa
Rosso with Kim Holland

The Kinky Boots Film, Milan
Exhibition (above)

Filming of 'Kinky Boots' the Movie

Steve, Margaret and Richard on Set

"Action!"
Steve Pateman Takes Over the
Director's Chair!

Filming of 'Kinky Boots' the Movie

Steve, Stan, Dan, Sara, Margaret and Richard

Kinky Boots End of Film Wrap Party Photo, 2005 Including After Show Pictures

Sophie Anderton and Steve

Joel Edgerton, Sara,
Chiwetel Ejiofor and
Sarah-Jane Potts

Dan Goes Celebrity Hunting at After Show Party!

Nick Frost and Dan

Jenni Falconer and Dan

Broadway Star from Kinky Boots Adinah Alexander Comes to Earls Barton
to Meet the Real-life Charlie Price at the Original Kinky Boots Factory

Mark, Tracy, Adinah Alexander, Liz and Colin Meet
at Kinky Boots Show in NYC

Steve, Sara and Dan at the London
Kinky Boots Premiere, 2015

Jerry Mitchell and Steve

London Kinky Boots After Show Party Pictures

Dan, Sara, Steve and Cyndi Lauper

Pictures of Contributors of Chapter XXVII

Jemima Rooper

Michele Kurland

The Kinky Boots Film 'Lauren' Meets
the Musical Kinky Boots 'Lauren'!

Sue Shepherd from 'Lacies'

Ellyn Marsh

Harvey Fierstein

Sarah-Jane Potts and Joel Edgerton

12

Nick Barton, Suzanne Mackie and
Peter Ettedgui from Harbour Pictures